LEADERSHIP GROWTH HACKS

LEADERSHIP GROWTH HACKS

A Guide for Emerging Leaders to Think Differently, Kick-Start Performance, and Get Ahead Quicker

BY DAVID BELMAN

Leadership Growth Hacks:
A Guide for Emerging Leaders to Think Differently,
Kick-Start Performance, and Get Ahead Quicker

Copyright © 2021 by David Belman

David Belman
1407 E. Sunset Drive
Waukesha, WI 53189
www.davidbelman.net

Library of Congress Cataloging-in-Publication Data
ISBN 978-1-7366398-0-1 (Paperback)
ISBN 978-1-7366398-1-8 (E-book)

Cover by Claire Lacy
Typesetting by Erin Campbell set in Macho and Beloved Sans

1 2 3 4 5 6 7 8 9 10

*To those meant for greatness, may this book be
a shining light in the dark to show you the way.*

TABLES OF CONTENTS

PREFACE

I was in the middle of a board meeting for the Wisconsin Builders Association and suddenly found myself riding an emotional high. The current secretary/treasurer needed to step down, which meant someone else needed to step up. Becoming a leader of an influential association was a key part to my long-term plan, and I was delighted by the unexpected opportunity to take on the responsibility sooner than I anticipated.

I was still basking in my good fortune when the next speaker entered the room. He was there to speak about Operation Finally Home, a philanthropic initiative that gave away mortgage-free homes to wounded veterans. My ears perked up.

I had first heard about the organization a year prior at an industry trade show. As a home builder, I was aware of all the cost, time, and hard work it takes to develop a new home. I was in awe of the magnitude of the charitable gift and humbled by all of the builders who had stepped up to lead past projects in other states. I knew instantly that I wanted to get involved, but when I left the trade show, life just kept going.

The speaker informed us that Operation Finally Home was looking to donate their next house in the Milwaukee area, where my company is based. As he gave his presentation, my heart pounded faster and faster. The passion I felt when I first learned about the organization came back full force. Sometimes life has a funny way of putting people in the right place at the right time. I wasn't quite ready for the opportunity the first time around, but it had come back around. This time it felt like a sign.

As the presentation ended, the speaker asked whether any of us would like to volunteer to lead the Milwaukee initiative. I looked around and could tell no one seemed keen to commit right then and there to giving away a free house. It would be a huge undertaking. I felt my hand go up before my head could even process it. This was a massive commitment—one of the biggest I had ever made. But I felt called to do it. Just an hour after accepting a new leadership position through the association, I was volunteering to give away a new home for free.

My brain raced the entire two-and-half-hour drive home. My first thought was, "Dad's going to kill me!" He founded our business and was in the process of phasing out while I took over, but he was definitely still involved and probably would have appreciated being consulted on such a large decision. How was he going to react when I told him what I had committed to? What would my wife say when I told her I had volunteered to work on a project that would take more time away from our family—without any financial reward for the sacrifice? And what would my team say when they found out they would be working on a time-consuming project that didn't drive profits for the business, a key metric for their compensation packages? On top of all that, the commitment to serving as president of the Wisconsin Builders Association would take even more time away from my current responsibilities for the next few years.

I drove on in silence as the feeling of dread grew bigger and bigger. I didn't regret volunteering; I knew Operation Finally Home was a worthwhile cause for servicemen and -women who had risked their lives for our country, and I was beyond excited to finally get involved. But now I was tasked with sharing my vision, gaining people's buy-in, and not messing this up.

Fast forward six years and my company has given away six free homes to wounded veterans through Operation Finally Home. In fact, it's what we're best known for in the industry. I didn't expect it at the time, but it was instrumental in my own personal growth as a leader.

By following my passion and taking a leap of faith, I inspired my team to go above and beyond. The initiative renewed their enthusiasm and love for their jobs, and we had a major boost in engagement and retention. We began winning all kinds of awards for the company culture we created and for our leadership within the industry. All of that momentum drew a lot of local attention, and sales skyrocketed. In an industry where differentiation is a challenge, philanthropy set us apart. And as it turned out, both my dad and my wife supported my decision from the get-go!

If you had asked me at the time how to drive exponential personal and organizational growth, my answer would not have been to give away a free home. But it was the answer I needed. Every time a wounded veteran and their family first see their brand-new, mortgage-free home that *we built*, I am beyond grateful for the decision I made all those years ago.

INTRODUCTION

I'm going to share a secret with you that I wish I had known when I was first starting out: those who work hardest don't necessarily get the biggest rewards. It would be nice if there were bonus points for doing things the hard way, but that isn't reality. People get ahead by working harder, but they get ahead faster by working smarter. When you become intentional about your actions, you will unlock your true potential. That's what this book is all about.

I started thinking about leadership early in life. I began working for my family's home development business when I was 17. As other kids prepared for college or worked summer jobs, I was entering a field that would become my lifelong career. As a second-generation home builder, I put a lot of pressure on myself to surpass people's expectations and earn my spot at the company.

Barely out of high school and with zero business experience, I felt lost. I learned a lot on the job through trial and error. My college business courses helped, but I soon found that most didn't hold a candle to what I learned in the field. It took decades of managing teams and growing my own company to realize that the things that matter most for personal and professional growth are actually quite simple—and they aren't necessarily what you'd expect.

We all want to become better at what we do. We want to learn more, advance our skills, be recognized, and achieve our dreams. But it can be overwhelming to think about all the things you want to accomplish and the skills necessary to do so. Where do you start? And what should you focus on first?

This book provides the direction you've been looking for. In addition to my own experience, I've interviewed leaders across a variety of fields to better understand how they reached success. By focusing on these growth-hacking strategies, you can take your career to the next level faster than you ever thought possible. The content is hyper-focused on what matters most and organized strategically so you can prioritize your efforts. From tackling fears to understanding mindset and how to craft systems that free up your time, we'll walk through a variety of leadership "hacks" that will change your life.

ACTION BEGETS OPPORTUNITY

Taking action leads to new growth opportunities you didn't even realize were available.

When I volunteered to lead a project for Operation Finally Home, it seemed impulsive, but the preparation required to tackle an endeavor of that magnitude actually began many years earlier.

I had been working on improving my leadership skills, and I had just gone through one of the biggest challenges I'd ever experienced. I was ready for more, so I decided to step up and take a risk. However, at the time, I had no idea how this project would accelerate my growth.

I felt passionate about the mission, but that wasn't enough; I had to portray that passion in a way that would inspire others to step up and volunteer. I found myself tasked with sharing my vision for the project with local business owners, city officials, and journalists to spread the word and persuade them to get on board. I was used to leading from my head, but this time I led from my heart. I got the opportunity to flex muscles I wasn't used to working, and I discovered strengths I didn't know I had. It seemed that every little aspect of the project created new opportunities for partnerships, friendships, and learning better ways to get things done. It wasn't smooth sailing every day, and we experienced a few setbacks along the way, but the project was instrumental in shaping who I am as a leader today.

You don't have to lead a massive project to hack your growth, but you will need to step outside your comfort zone and take action. Once you gain momentum, you'll find that individual efforts create even more opportunities. Maybe you'll go above and beyond on a project and, due to your success, you're immediately asked to lead another. Or you'll forge a new relationship through networking and your new connection introduces you to their contacts. There truly is a butterfly effect to personal and professional growth. Everything is connected, and every step you take is one step closer to the person you want to become.

I believe in you. By picking up this book, you've already shown that you are capable of being—and doing—more. You feel a calling to take your career to the next level. You're action oriented, and you know that it takes intentionality to bridge the gap between where you are now and where you want to be. This desire for change and your disposition for taking action create the perfect baseline for growth-hacking success. As I share the skills to kick-start your career, know that you're already positioned to put my advice into practice and drive real change that you can be proud of. I look forward to going on this growth-hacking journey with you!

CHAPTER 1

OVERCOMING FEAR

It was 11 AM on a gorgeous Friday morning in May. The sun was shining, the trees were starting to blossom, and it seemed like everyone at the office that morning had taken a collective exhalalation, thankful that the frigid Wisconsin winter was finally coming to an end. It would have been a great day to play hooky, but my team and I had a ton of work to do.

For home developers, spring is a busy season. People like to start construction early so they can be finished before winter. I was putting in a lot of overtime, and I had been in the office since 7 AM that morning just trying to keep up with the influx of projects. As I thought about how much I'd rather be outside enjoying the unseasonably warm weather, my business partner strolled in, making his first appearance in two days.

As a leader of the company, I made it my goal to arrive at the office as early as I expected my employees to. I wanted to set an example and show the team that I wasn't asking them to do anything I wouldn't do. But my partner saw things differently. After 14 years in business, instead of taking on the responsibility to set the right example, he used his leadership role as permission to do whatever he wanted.

Over the past several years, he had become increasingly less engaged in the company's operations. This wasn't noticeable in the beginning. Instead of coming in at 8 AM, he'd get there at 9 AM. Then 9 AM turned into 10 AM, and so on. His lunch breaks got longer as well. He wasn't an eat-at-your-desk kind of guy, which was fine. But it was a bold move to come in a couple hours late, take a 90-minute lunch break, work on a few personal things, and then dip out early.

In the summer, he began leaving early to go waterskiing. He would drive to the office with the boat trailer attached to his truck so he could head straight to the lake. I heard the "must be nice" whispers from our employees, and I felt bad about what was happening. They had grown especially bitter ever since my partner had hired a close friend to fill a sales role and had routinely given him special treatment. The team saw through this deception whenever they would leave the office together, boat trailer in tow, saying they were going out to "inspect a new property."

Perhaps all of that would have been fine if my partner was still performing at the same level as when we began. He and I shared ownership of the company and split the profits 50/50, so it was a reasonable expectation that we'd also split the work. When his contributions declined, I didn't mind because I valued our relationship and I didn't want to rock the boat. But it got to the point where it seemed like he wasn't even trying. I was bringing in two to three times the volume of business that he was, and I was starting to feel taken advantage of.

But the bigger problem was how this affected our team. I was the leader they had access to on a regular basis, and I was the one who answered their questions, gave them direction, and took the heat when there was a problem. My partner was never around when important decisions were made, so he became less and less involved in the day-to-day operations. But when he found out we made plans to move forward with a project in a certain way, he would get mad that he wasn't consulted. He'd throw his weight around and give the team alternative orders just to feel significant. It created an awkward situation in the office. Direction flip-flopped repeatedly, and people wasted a lot of time redoing work. It was terrible for morale.

The seriousness of the situation took a while to sink in. Let me rephase that: it took *years* to sink it. During that time, I continued to show up every day, trying to raise the bar for the company, improve the culture, and grow the business. But in the back on my mind, I knew we were on a negative trajectory due to my partner's actions. It was clear that he was no longer mentally or emotionally invested in our organization's success, and the smartest thing to do would be to part ways.

Running a business can be tough, but it helps if you step back and look at key decisions in very black-and-white terms. Will your change benefit the company and its key stakeholders? Letting a small issue fester can cause financial hardship, and a large issue could lead to closing a business in the future. Though good markets can cover up bad habits, all it takes is one bad market and one bad decision and everything you worked toward is gone. Ask yourself, "Who does that benefit?" There likely are many people relying on you, and if your company is no longer around, how many people will be affected? As a leader, you have to look at the long term and be willing to make tough decisions for your company's survival.

I decided to either buy him out of the company or dissolve the whole thing and start a new venture on my own. This would have been difficult for partners in any business, but in our case, it was worse because we were family. Even if we went our separate ways in business, we would still sit across from each other at the table during holiday meals.

The gravity of severing our business relationship—and potentially our personal relationship—consumed my brain for weeks, then months, then years. Finally, I realized that avoiding conflict was only prolonging my suffering. My employees suffered as well, as did our business's bottom line. Ignoring the problem wasn't going to fix it. The only option was to tackle it head-on. I don't think I've ever been more afraid of anything in my life, but I realized I couldn't grow as a person or a business owner until I found a way to overcome this. I thought about what I wanted to say to him and asked him to meet to discuss some important things about the business.

He didn't take it well. To be honest, our relationship kind of blew up for a while. Some of our family members wanted to stay out of it, whereas others had strong opinions that they made well known. Eventually, my partner came around and agreed to let me buy him out. Deep down, he knew he wasn't happy at the company, and I'm sure he was ultimately relieved to finally have an out.

When he stepped down from the business, it felt like a dark cloud had been lifted. In just the first week, there were more smiles, more laughter, and, most importantly, more sales than there had been in a long time. We sold four homes that week, and things only improved. The vibe around the office totally transformed, and we became more cohesive and productive than we ever had been. We began winning awards for our company culture and our work in the building industry.

It took me years to tackle the thing I had been dreading most, yet I knew almost instantly I made the right choice. Even though it was painful in the moment, I realized that with all my worrying, I had built it up into something bigger than it actually was. The pain I experienced stressing out about the situation and worrying about confrontation was much worse than living through the actual event.

Has something like this ever happened to you? Have you ever avoided something—or put it off indefinitely—because of fear? Perhaps it's something small, like learning a new skill. Maybe you'd love to become a better singer or basketball player but you're afraid of looking stupid. Or it could be that you're avoiding an honest conversation with someone because you're concerned that they won't take it well. Or maybe you want to shift the direction of your career but you're afraid of losing everything you worked for.

Fear is the number-one impediment to growth. There are millions of things to be afraid of in this world, but unless those fears are keeping you from physical harm, they probably aren't serving you. When you're afraid, you retreat into yourself. You avoid trying new things. You get stuck in a negative mindset where you can't see the opportunities that could come from change. This is a dangerous place to be. You can get trapped in a state of fear for years and miss out on opportunities to shape your dream life.

FAILURE IS GOOD

In order to accelerate your growth, we first need to tackle fear. To grow as a professional, and as a human being, you must change. But change can be scary. It pushes you outside your comfort zone, and though it can present plenty of positive opportunities, it can also increase your chances of failure. After all, it's hard to reach perfection on your first try.

For high achievers, this can be the most difficult aspect of growth: fear of failure. Those used to performing above their peers don't always welcome the idea of having one of their efforts totally flop. A single failure can seem devastating, but it doesn't have to be that way.

I'm going to tell you something that might be hard to hear: *failure is good.* You learn from failure. To learn how to do something right, sometimes you first have to do it wrong. Every business owner or leader fails at something almost every single day. Top performers are able to learn from failure, make the necessary adjustments, and do something different.

If you let fear keep you from trying new things, you'll miss out on important lessons that could open up the next phase of your career. Always push yourself. You might not feel yourself plateauing, but if you aren't pushing forward and taking smart risks, you aren't progressing at your full potential.

It can be difficult to know where to apply your efforts, especially when the places that need the most work are hardest to acknowledge. What skill sets and competencies don't come naturally for you? Those areas are probably where most of your fears lie.

Developing skills outside our natural abilities can feel like a lost cause. We all hold limiting beliefs about ourselves. Many of them stem from childhood. Being picked last in gym, flunking tests, being made fun of, or listening to friends and family members tell us we aren't cut out for something can bruise our sense of self-worth for years.

If you let others' opinions shape the way you view yourself, you will miss out on opportunities to develop skills that could turn into real talents. One reason for this is clear: no one can become truly great at something without practice. Not a single one of us comes out of the womb batting .300 or speaking three fluent languages. It's true that some talents are easy to identify early on, but there are so many skill sets that we don't even get a chance to tap into until we're much older.

One of my friends was convinced she was terrible at public speaking. It caused her a great deal of anxiety, and she assumed she would never be good at it. The reality was that she had only given a couple group presentations in her entire life. Her lack of confidence caused her to avoid speaking in front of groups. Over the years, as her peers got better at presenting, she found herself lagging behind. It became her Achilles heel. Once she realized it was impacting her career, she decided to step out of her comfort zone and become a better speaker. She was surprised at how many resources she found, including books on structuring interesting presentations, YouTube videos on how to captivate audiences, and Meetup groups to practice and get feedback. She realized that the people she thought were naturally gifted speakers had actually been honing their craft for years. When she understood that she wasn't hardwired to be a bad presenter, her outlook transformed. It was no longer an emotional battle; it was simply a matter of putting in the effort to practice.

There's a popular model that illustrates the journey of learning something new. In the first stage, Unconsciously Incompetent, you don't have a certain skill, and you don't recognize that you lack it. In the second stage, Consciously Incompetent, you gain awareness. You understand the value of learning a particular skill, and you also recognize your deficit at mastering it. This stage can be painful, which is why people often get stuck here. But if you put in the practice and hard work, you become Consciously Competent, meaning you know how to do something but the skill still requires your concentration. In the final stage of learning, Unconsciously Competent, you become so good at something that you don't even have to think about doing it.

You've made this journey countless times over the course of your life, whether it's riding a bike, cooking a meal, or changing your child's diapers. As a working professional, you will continue to make this journey throughout your career. In the beginning, it's a little intimidating to run sales meetings, conduct performance reviews, or give status updates to your boss. But after a while, you get over your jitters and it becomes second nature. The key is to remember that you will get better with more time on task.

I experienced this recently when I partnered with a few other entrepreneurs to create an organization called The Young Guns Movement. Our goal is to inspire leaders of all ages to be innovative, break the conventional rules of business, and push for their full potential. We create a lot of content through Young Guns, including live events, virtual events, and a YouTube channel called YGTV, but it didn't all start out perfectly.

When I began hosting a new show on YGTV, the crew and I went through the four stages of competency. Looking back at the first recording, it was a little rough! We were confident in the content, but we didn't realize that we had some issues with the camera angles and other aspects of the production. We quickly became conscious of what needed to improve, and the show began running more smoothly. I loosened up as I got comfortable in front of the camera, and the latest episodes are light-years beyond the first ones we recorded. It just goes to show that you can't give up and give in to fear if you don't do something perfect the first time.

Michaela Alexis, who spoke at our Young Guns Annual Summit, knows about overcoming failure and refusing to give up. She decided to audition for TEDx, one of the top speaking opportunities in the world, but it didn't go quite as planned. On stage, Michaela was surprised at how the bright lights prevented her from seeing the audience. She was used to taking visual cues from the audience when she spoke, and the stage lights threw her off. She froze, forgetting everything she was going to say. Luckily, she had her notes in her pocket, but her performance was shaky at best. TEDx talks are known for their high level of professionalism and quality of presentation. Can you imagine seeing one of their speakers pull out and read from a crumpled piece of paper? To Michaela's credit, she finished her talk, but as soon as she finished, she ran offstage and cried in her car.

Then, instead of accepting defeat, she decided to contact the TEDx committee and ask for her audition tape so she could share it online as a lesson about overcoming failure. The committee was shocked she would want the tape, but they gave it to her. When she posted about her failure on LinkedIn, it went viral! And even better, the committee contacted Michaela and asked her to come back to the audition site and give a talk to high-school students about perseverance. Since then, her career has grown exponentially and her business is flourishing. Her progress has been inspirational to the YG community.

EXERCISE: IDENTIFY YOUR TOP FEARS

Fears hold you back from personal growth. Ask yourself the questions below to help brainstorm and identify fears you should tackle head-on. Afterward, use the APART Method™ below to get unstuck and move forward.

— *What would you do differently if you weren't afraid?*
— *Is there a tough conversation that needs to be had to move a challenge in the right direction?*
— *Is there something that's been weighing on your mind but you keep pushing off?*
— *What would you try to achieve if failure wasn't an option?*
— *What would need to change for you to transform your daily reality into your dream life?*
— *Is there something you think you aren't good at but haven't had much time practicing?*

> — *Is there a skill you admire in other people that you would like to have as well?*

THE APART METHOD: TEAR YOUR FEAR APART!

Aware — Be aware that fear exists and understand where it originates.

Plan — Create a plan to tackle the issue step by step. Break your fear into smaller parts so it doesn't seem as daunting.

Analyze — Identify all of the positive things that will result from overcoming your fear. What will you gain? Talk with someone about what you are going through and have them keep you accountable.

Reprogram — Use visualization to reprogram your way of thinking to stop associating pain with fear. Instead, focus on the outcome—moving past your fear—and how great you will feel when you overcome it.

Take Action — Nothing kills fear faster than taking action and facing it head-on. The fear is always worse in your mind than it is in real life.

Avoiding change only prolongs the suffering. I'm reminded of an old Russian saying about a guy who knows his dog's tail is injured and needs to be amputated. He feels terrible about having to lop it off, so he cuts off one inch every day until it's gone. Half measures only will lead to more pain. Sometimes you have to just chop it off and move forward.

We're all afraid of different things, but how we handle that fear makes all the difference. Proactively facing the difficult parts of life and taking on what scares you most is not an easy feat. But you'll be a better person for it, and you'll free yourself up to focus on bigger and better things.

CHAPTER 2

HACKING YOUR MINDSET

What if you could manifest your dreams just by thinking the right thoughts? It may sound like science fiction or fantasy, but the reality is that we are only beginning to understand the power of the human brain. Don't get me wrong—I'm not suggesting that you pour your energy into envisioning yourself winning the lottery, but there is value in becoming more intentional about your thoughts.

Perhaps you've heard of the Law of Attraction, which is the theory that positive or negative thoughts drive positive or negative experiences in a person's life. This concept was made famous in books like *Think and Grow Rich* by Napoleon Hill, which has sold more than 100 million copies since 1937, and *The Secret* by Rhonda Byrne, which has sold more than 30 million copies since 2006.[1,2] Whether readers of these books end up believing wholeheartedly that mastering their thoughts is the key to controlling their destiny, the high volume in sales certainly shows that plenty of people are interested in exploring the power of their mind.

I want to focus on mindset early in our journey together because it's the quickest way for you to grow as a leader and provides a solid foundation for personal development. When you master your mindset, anything is possible. It takes hard work and continual effort, but it is well worth it.

The body is a servant to the mind. The vast majority of your actions are driven by your subconscious, which is like an echo chamber for the conscious mind. You can control your conscious mind, either through positive or negative thoughts, and your subconscious will reinforce those thoughts by playing them back in a constant loop. When you think certain thoughts, your subconscious follows suit, and soon you're feeling the emotions associated with those thoughts and taking actions that are in line with your feelings.

A great example of the interaction between the conscious and the unconscious is the placebo effect. When people believe they will feel healthier, they often do. It's a phenomenon that's widely accepted, and it's the Law of Attraction in action. With this in mind, it shouldn't come as a surprise that being intentional about your thoughts can totally change your life.

One of the biggest shifts in my success—both in my life and in business—was when I made a conscious effort to reprogram my mind. I realized how much my subconscious impacted who I was and the opportunities available to me. So I worked on improving my mindset in a variety of ways.

One of the most effective methods I found was implementing positive self-talk every day. I thought about my weaknesses and what I wanted to improve upon, and I started telling myself that I was already good at those things. I mentally repeated my daily mantra: "I am a great delegator." This helped me keep delegating top of mind, and I started to notice more and more opportunities to enlist my team for help. Telling myself I was good at delegating helped me notice all the times when I was successful at it, and that boosted my confidence. Over time, these small changes made a huge difference in my results, and today, I actually pride myself in my ability to delegate.

As powerful as the subconcious brain is, it has a hard time processing negative instructions. When I created my mantra, I didn't phrase it as, "I need to stop taking on too much work." Instead, I phrased it as a positive affirmation about my own capabilities.

Now, for the next few seconds, try not to think about penguins on roller-skates...

How'd you do?

By thinking about something you want to avoid, you generally end up fixating on it. That's why you have to use positive instead of negative phrasing in your mantras and self-talk. Instead of telling yourself, "Don't eat sugar," instead say, "I eat healthy foods that nourish my body." This switches your attention away from sugar and toward healthy foods. It might seem like a minor distinction, but it's powerful.

If you're constantly thinking about sugar—regardless of whether you intend on eating it—you're going to see it everywhere. You'll constantly drive past delicious bakeries, there will be doughnuts at every meeting, and when you hear someone say "gimme a break," you'll find yourself craving a candy bar.

Sometimes it's difficult to focus positive thoughts on your abilities. This is especially true if you've received criticism on your work or you sense that your boss or colleagues have doubts about your ability to perform. Low self-esteem and a lack of confidence affects your mindset, and if you don't nip those emotions in the bud, it impacts your performance as well.

I met Morgan Markowski as she was just starting her career selling supplemental insurance. She connected with me on LinkedIn, and I become her first client. Her boss also came to our initial meeting, and it was clear from the beginning that his main strategy was to boldly and assertively ask for the sale. Even though Morgan had made the appointment with me, he barely let her speak. As he rambled on and on, I felt bad because I could see Morgan was uncomfortable with his process. It didn't fit her personality—or mine for that matter.

It was her first real job, and she was just learning. Her boss obviously had very low confidence in her, and I could tell she felt unsure of herself as well. With a manager like that, who wouldn't feel deflated? Her first big job was going to go south quickly if she didn't learn how to get out from under the negative influence of her boss.

After our first meeting, Morgan reached out to me for some help and advice. I routinely mentor students and find it to be rewarding, so I carved out some time for her. After getting to know her a bit, I saw a lot of myself in her when I was just learning to sell homes. She had a lot of drive, but she needed some sales skills and a good dose of self-confidence. I offered to teach her a few things, and we primarily focused on mindset. To succeed in any role—especially sales—she first needed to believe in herself.

Morgan started implementing positive self-talk into her daily routine. She also created a vision board featuring photos and magazine cutouts representing what her life would be like when she achieved her goals. Most importantly, she shifted her mindset from worrying about her performance to being excited about doing great things.

"I started being a lot nicer to myself, and I realized that what I put into my mind is what I get back," Morgan said. "I began to start my day with gratitude and pay more attention to the voices in my head to make sure I was talking to myself more positively."

Right away, she began closing more deals. Her boss and other leaders in the company took note. It wasn't long before she was awarded top new salesperson in the company. Shortly thereafter, she was promoted to become a recruiter and team lead.

I couldn't be happier about the progress Morgan made in just a year. Her career is in a completely different place, and the foundation for that change was her mindset. When she truly believed she could accomplish her goals, she succeeded. That's the beauty of mindset hacks.

Here are a few ways you can master your mindset:

- *Let go of beliefs that hold you back:* You might not realize you have beliefs about yourself that just aren't true. For example, if you've never been a runner, you might think you aren't cut out for it. Every time you try to run, you're gasping for air and want to go home after half a mile. But what would happen if you believed you would improve? Would you be inspired to run just a little farther every day? You might surprise yourself as your endurance and speed grow over time. Before you know it, you're running miles and miles and feeling like a million bucks, and all because you focused on your ability to progress. The basis for improving everything in your life is believing you can do it. Believe you are the best person to handle each of your responsibilities, tasks, and clients. Believe you work for the best company with the best product.

- *Let go of the people that hold you back:* Sometimes people don't want you to change. People are conditioned to like homeostasis. They don't want things to change. They are insecure about themselves and their own success, and they don't want to be left behind. If you have people like that in your life, it might be time to distance yourself from them. Surround yourself with positive people who believe in you, cheer you on, and fully support you in achieving your goals and improving your life.

- *Create a vision board:* Close your eyes and imagine if you got everything you wanted. What does success look like for you? Would you be driving a Lamborghini, taking lavish vacations in Europe, or enjoying hours of free time each day to spend however you please? Maybe all of the above? Focusing on what you really want in life will help you keep your eye on the prize. Create a collage that represents your dream life and hang it where you will see it every day.

- *Identify three things you're grateful for every day:* Tune your mind toward positivity. When you're trying to grow yourself as a leader, this is the fastest way to do it. People want to help those who are positive and grateful. If you can exhibit those qualities, people will go out of their way to make sure you are successful. As an example, think about giving a piece of candy to two different kids. One greedily snatches it from your hand, while the other smiles, thanks you, and can't stop bragging about that tasty piece of candy. The next time you have a piece of candy, which kid are you more likely to treat?

- *Practice five daily affirmations:* Come up with five positive statements that reflect your goals and/or something you want to improve (e.g., "I am a confident and engaging presenter."). Repeat each affirmation out loud to yourself. Take deep breaths while you do this and visualize yourself succeeding. When you really get in the zone, this practice can almost be enchanting. Over time, your belief will grow and begin to reshape your reality.

GOALS

A positive mindset puts you on the right path and makes your goals crystal clear. Goals help focus your energy on what matters most. Make goal setting a formal process. It's difficult to hold yourself accountable if you can't set specific deadlines. A vague idea isn't enough to provide a solid understanding of what it will take to reach your goal.

I recommend the rule of 1•3•90: plan one year out, focus on three goals at a time, and break progress into 90-day segments. This system works because it helps us plan for big-picture goals in smaller chunks, taking something that could be overwhelming and making it manageable. "How do you eat an elephant?" one of my mentors used to ask. "One bite at a time." This is the perfect mindset for achieving goals. Small actions add up to big changes.

I included an example of the goal sheet I developed for my team. To download a free, editable version of this goals chart, go to www.davidbelman.net/resources/goals. Fill this out for all three of your goals so that you have a solid plan for moving forward. This is crucial for success. Without a plan, you're basically lost at sea with a rickety boat and no map. Your goals will provide the map and the compass to guide you to shore. Not identifying the small steps you need to take along the way leads to lost time sitting around doing nothing instead of taking action toward meaningful progress. Once you create your plan, all you have to do is FOCUS: follow one course until successful.

No one is immune to negative emotions. Hacking your mindset takes belief, conscious energy, and consistency. Don't let self-doubt and negativity creep in. It's essential that you work to keep those thoughts at bay. They will hold you back.

Take time every day to cultivate a positive, grateful, glass-is-half-full outlook. You will bring better people and opportunities into your life. Over time, this will shift the way you view the world—and the way other people see you.

GOAL SHEET

TODAY'S DATE :

GOAL TYPE: _____   PERSONAL -or- BUSINESS

GOAL #1: _____

_____

Make all goals SMART (specific, measurable, attainable, results, time centered)

POTENTIAL CHALLENGES	POTENTIAL SOLUTIONS

KEY ACTIONS TO COMPLETE GOAL	TARGET DATE	COMPLETION DATE
1.		
2.		
3.		
4.		
5.		

CHAPTER 3

LEARNING TO SPEAK THEIR LANGUAGE

After graduating high school, I began working full time for my family business. I was excited to begin my career while going to college, but I soon realized I had a lot to learn. I started out in a sales role, working directly with home buyers to showcase our properties, conduct tours, and provide the information they needed to make one of the biggest purchasing decisions of their lives. For me, a regular day on the job was often a major day in the lives of my customers.

One of the very first things I learned in my new role was the different ways people behave when making decisions. Some customers peppered me with questions about everything from interiors to warranties, others asked very little, and a surprising number seemed to care more about me, my background, and my family business than they did about the houses we sold. As I led people through the properties, some listened intently as I described the features in each room. Others ignored me as they opened and closed drawers, flipped light switches, and flushed the toilets. A handful of buyers knew they wanted to purchase within a few minutes of seeing a new property, whereas others took months of deliberation across multiple visits.

As I communicated with this diverse group of home buyers, it became clear my messaging was hit or miss. The exact same information and delivery could either instantly build rapport or totally fail to make an impression, like I was speaking another language. That's why I initially found the sales experience so facinating—and so incredibly frustrating! How could I get better at communicating with customers if I couldn't discern what they cared about?

Over the next few years, I focused on listening and observing. I began to see patterns in how people behaved, and I could predict what kind of messaging would resonate best. I took cues from my college psychology classes, and I adjusted my communication style to relate with customers on a deeper level. Slowly but surely, I got better at recognizing what mattered to buyers, and my sales numbers took off.

Fast-forward about 16 years and I was still focused on better understanding my customers. One of my mentors recommended I look into personality assessment tools. There's a ton on the market, but the DISC assessment was one of his favorites. As soon as I started learning about DISC's four main personality types, I began picturing specific people for each one. I could see my friends, family members, customers, and even myself in the descriptions. Over the years, I had been observing people, listening to them, and tailoring my communication to "speak their language," but learning about DISC took things to the next level. I finally had a guide for classifying personalities and behaviors, along with specific insights on how each of the four types makes decisions.

I found the DISC personality profiles so accurate that I built them into part of my hiring process. I hire for personality over skill. Skills can be taught; personality is harder to change. DISC made it easier to hire the right people. In fact, I no longer interview job candidates until they've taken a DISC assessment and I've reviewed how well their personality is likely to align with what's needed. This process allows me to successfully fit new hires with roles that suit them while reinforcing company culture.

It's been seven years since I learned about DISC, and my business is in a totally different place because of it. DISC helps me communicate better with customers, motivates my employees, and connects me with people from all walks of life in a way that builds trust and rapport. That's why I'm so excited to share this tool with you!

No matter what industry or role you're in, you will benefit from learning how different types of people perceive the world and make decisions. There will always be someone you want to influence. Whether it's gaining buy-in from colleagues on a new endeavor, persuading your partner to watch the movie you want to see, or negotiating a salary increase, knowing how to influence different types of people will make it easier for you to get the things you want.

THE DISC ASSESSMENT

The DISC assessment splits people into four basic behavioral types: direct, influential, steady, or calculating. There are two basic questions to consider when it comes to personality and behavior that will allow you to determine which type you're dealing with.

- *Outgoing vs. reserved:* If someone is talkative and proactively engaged, they're probably outgoing, which would make them a direct or influential personality. If they are shy and don't approach right away, they are probably reserved and either a steady or calculating personality.

Once you have figured out if they are outgoing or reserved, you next need to determine if they are primarily task-focused or people-focused.

- *Task-focused vs. people-focused:* If someone talks about themself, their family, or friends or asks you about yourself and the people in your life, they are people-focused, which means that they are either influential or steady. If instead they focus on the details of a transaction, they are task-focused, which means that they are either a direct or calculating personality.

Once you make the determination of outgoing vs. reserved and task-focused vs. people-focused, you can determine their primary personality trait. This becomes extremely valuable information in order to fine-tune your approach to the people you communicate with.

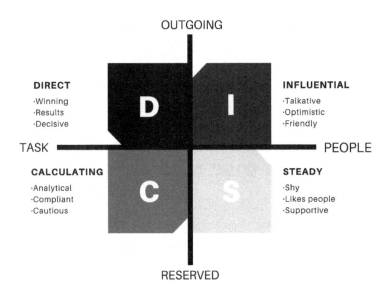

To read this chart: Above the horizontal line are the outgoing personality types, direct and influential. Below the horizontal line are the reserved personality types, calculating and steady. On the verticle line, the left side is for the task-orientated personality types, direct and calculating. On the right side are the people-oriented personality types, influential and steady. When you can quickly diagnose the outgoing vs. reserved and then the task vs. people question, you can quickly determine someone's primary personality type and put it to use.

Once you can identify personality types, the next step is understanding what is important to personality and how you should adjust your approach to best influence them.

DIRECT (OUTGOING/TASK-FOCUSED)

- *Embraces challenge*
- *Decisive*
- *Assertive*

LIKES:

- Short communication
- Change
- Getting to the point
- Newest, first, or best
- Results

DISLIKES:

- Talking about feelings
- Long explanations
- Big reports
- Not being in control

IN ACTION:

- At a party: will barge right in, introduce themselves, and talk to a bunch of different people.
- Getting in the pool: will see how far they can jump or will want to be the first to get in.
- Careers: professional athletes, CEOs, business owners

HOW TO PERSUADE:
(EASIEST OF ALL PERSONALITIES TO INFLUENCE!)

- Get to the point.
- Don't waste their time.
- Show them the bottom line or how your proposal will help them win or beat the competition.
- Be professional and efficient.
- Once the agreement is made, stop talking.

Celebrity profile: Michael Jordan, General George S. Patton, Arnold Schwarzenegger, Donald Trump

INFLUENTIAL (OUTGOING/PEOPLE-FOCUSED)

— *Talkative*
— *Optimistic*
— *Wants to be connected with others*

LIKES:

- Socializing
- Having fun
- Recognition and approval
- Making sure everyone is getting along
- Working with their friends or becoming friends

DISLIKES:

- A lot of detail
- Long or repetitive tasks
- Being left out

IN ACTION:

- At a party: wants to be the center of the attention and will be seen in the middle of a large group of people talking.
- Getting in the pool: if everyone else is in the pool, they are too.
- Careers: greeters, radio or TV hosts, networkers, receptionists

HOW TO PERSUADE:
(SECOND EASIEST TO INFLUENCE)

- Be friendly.
- Ask about their family and friends.
- Play up the emotional side of your offer.
- Avoid a lot of details or explanations.
- Talk about how you are going to celebrate together.
- Tell stories.
- Talk about the ongoing relationship.

Celebrity profile: Ryan Seacrest, Oprah, Dolly Parton, Ellen

STEADY (RESERVED/PEOPLE-FOCUSED)

- *Shy, soft-spoken*
- *Enjoys being around people*
- *Supportive and caring*
- *Relaxed disposition*

- *Empathetic*
- *Stable*
- *Patient*

LIKES:

- Processes and systems
- Going at their own pace
- Knowing what's next
- A schedule or routine
- Repetition
- Tranquility

DISLIKES:

- Change
- Surprises
- Pressure tactics
- Risks
- Confrontation

IN ACTION:

- At a party: they will be off to the side smiling at someone or in a close conversation with a person they know for most of the evening.
- At a pool: they will dip a toe in, then slowly put their leg in, then sit in the water, then climb in and finally swim around.
- Careers: factory workers, nurses, machine operators, drivers, coaches

HOW TO PERSUADE:
(HARDER TO INFLUENCE AND WILL TAKE MORE TIME)

- Be friendly and polite.
- Speak slower.
- Provide clear next steps.
- Use a simple, steady process.
- Don't force them into anything.
- Take time to build rapport.
- Be their advisor and walk them through the process.

Celebrity profile: Mother Teresa, Mr. Rogers, Michael J. Fox, Justin Timberlake, Barack Obama

CALCULATING (RESERVED/TASK-FOCUSED)

- *Serious*
- *Formal*
- *Analytical*

- *Compliant*
- *Dependable*
- *Cautious*

LIKES:

- Research, reports, and doing homework
- Accuracy/perfection
- Data
- Clear rules and guidelines

DISLIKES:

- Chitchat
- Spontaneity
- Feelings—especially irrational ones
- Ambiguity

IN ACTION:

- At a party: They would rather be at home. Most likely will be at a quiet part of the party sitting at a table watching everyone.
- Getting in the pool: they will ask the temperature, how often the water is treated, what the chlorine and pH levels are, and then double check the weather before going in.
- Careers: accountants, financial investors, engineers, attorneys

HOW TO PERSUADE:
(HARDEST TO INFLUENCE)

- Don't be overly social or friendly.
- They want data, so explain the features and details.
- Provide comparisons to other options.
- Whenever possible, provide research, articles, or other resources that have more information.
- Prepare for your conversation and be accurate.
- Don't rush.

Celebrity profile: Bill Gates, Alan Greenspan, Mr. Spock

Personality is multidimensional and can change over time with concious effort. Your primary behaviors can be influenced depending on whether you are feeling comfortable or under pressure. People also have a natural and an adapted personality, and their behavior can change depending on the state they are in. Your natural state is how you act when you are relaxed—for example, how you are around your friends and family. Your adapted state is when you are under pressure, like facing an important deadline at work. Your DISC levels predictably shift when you are in different states. If you are under pressure, you may talk faster or you may slow down and get very quiet.

People's sudden shifts in behavior are great cues in selling situations. Listen closely and observe to pick up on the nuances. If you can pick up on these subtle shifts, you gain a powerful opportunity to match their behavior and earn their trust. Developing this skill will also help you increase your empathy, another great skill of an emerging leader.

It is impossible to understand others if you don't understand yourself. That's why I always recommend people take their own DISC assessment. The best free option I've found online is through www.truity.com.

Once you understand what makes you tick, it's easier to see how other people are alike or different. This knowledge helps in a variety of ways. First and foremost, it gives you another perspective. For example, if you're a direct personality and you make decisions quickly, you might not understand that some people are simply not wired that way, and that type of pressure could be extremely detrimental. You will always get better results if you adapt your style to the person you're working with using the language and techniques outlined earlier. This knowledge alone can make a noticeable impact on your professional and personal life.

DISC EXERCISE

Reflect on what you've learned about the different personalities. Do you know people who clearly fit one of the four types? If so, identify a couple things you could do differently to better communicate with them in the future. It's incredibly helpful to put yourself in another person's shoes and try to see the world through their eyes.

VAK LEARNING STYLES

To understanding yourself and others, you also need to understand learning styles. Small changes in communication can greatly impact how your message is received. Most people are one of three types: visual learners, auditory learners, or kinesthetic learners. If you want to teach someone, you will get the best results by tailoring your message to their learning style. By tapping into how someone's brain naturally processes information, you can present your points in a way that will leave a lasting impression.

Luckily, picking up on learning styles is easier than you think. With a little practice, you often can pick up on someone's learning style within minutes of meeting them. Included below is a short guide on what to look for and how to change your messaging for the three different types of learners.

VISUAL

- 60% of the population

- Learns from written communication, notes, pictures, diagrams, and charts

- Remembers faces rather than names

- Thinks in pictures

HOW TO IDENTIFY:

- Looks around frequently to take in their surroundings

- Tends to wear nice clothes, clean in appearance (will even wear something uncomfortable just to be in style)

- Uses words that relate to vision (e.g., "I would like to see...," "May I view...," "I'm just looking...")

HOW TO BEST COMMUNICATE WITH THEM:

- Use photos, visual aids, and videos

- Invite them to see things in person

- Use words related to vision (e.g., "Are you seeing this as a good solution?")

AUDITORY

- 10% of the population

- Learns by hearing others talk and explain

- Written information has little meaning until heard

- Distracted by noises

- Remembers by listening (especially with music)

HOW TO IDENTIFY:

- Often prefers phone over email or text

- Talks while doing things

- Uses words related to hearing (e.g., "I would like to hear more...," "Sounds like a plan...," "Tell me more...")

HOW TO BEST COMMUNICATE WITH THEM:

- Share stories of similar experiences

- Talk them through your process

- Use words that relate to hearing (e.g., "Would you like to hear more? May I explain this to you?")

KINESTHETIC

- 30% of population

- Learns through touch and movement

- Remembers what is done rather than what is seen or heard

HOW TO IDENTIFY:

- Gets physically involved

- Enjoys activity or playing games

- Tends to prioritize comfort over style when it comes to their shoes and clothes

- Uses words related to touch and experience (e.g., "I like how this feels...," "My gut tells me...," "I have a good feeling about this...")

HOW TO BEST COMMUNICATE WITH THEM:

- Let them try things out

- Do demonstrations that allow them to actively participate

- Use words related to touch and experience (e.g., "How does this feel to you?")

Over the years, I've practiced and honed my communication skills to better connect with different learning styles, and it makes a huge difference in becoming truly influential. Now when I'm showing properties to home buyers, I know when to invite certain people to jump up and down and feel how solid the floors are and when to encourage others to take plenty of photos during a tour. For auditory learners, I make sure to tell them stories of other clients' experiences and how we were able to help them. It may sound like a minor thing, but you would be amazed at the difference it makes in driving meaningful and memorable interactions with people.

DEEPENING YOUR AWARENESS

Influencing others is complicated. Everyone has a different perception of the world. What seems logical to you may be completely foreign to someone else. In order to relate to all kinds of people, you need to increase your awareness.

I firmly believe God gave us two ears and one mouth for a reason. Listening is the basis for connecting at a deeper level, and it's the only way to effectively assess and respond to different personality and learning types. But the reality is that most people aren't very good at listening! Instead of truly focusing on what someone has to say, people get distracted, they focus on what they're going to say next, and they miss clues as to what's really important to the person who is speaking.

Poor listening is detrimental to relationships, whether with people you're meeting for the first time or loved ones who have been in your life for decades. As you focus on personal growth and development, improving your listening skills is a great way to better understand those around you.

With some deliberate practice, you can work on specific areas and change the way you're showing up so that you can better connect with others. Reflect on your own personality and learning type and how it impacts your performance at work and in your personal life. Do some additional research on DISC and VAK and identify how your traits can be strengths or weaknesses in various situations. (Many DISC reports will give you this information.)

I used to be shy and reserved. I was nervous speaking in front of people, and I always avoided the spotlight. But to grow as a leader, I knew I needed to be outgoing and personable. So I worked on it and tried hard to push myself out of my comfort zone. It took some determination to overcome those fears, but it shaped me into a more well-rounded person, and it gave me the skills I needed to connect with colleagues and clients to grow my business.

Thinking back to the previous chapter, you may find an opportunity to create a mantra around improving one of your weaknesses. You might also choose to come up with a goal to get out of your comfort zone and work some new muscles. As you work on yourself and become more aware of your world view, you will gain a greater insight into the motivations and needs of those around you.

CHAPTER 4

BECOMING MORE EFFICIENT

Have you ever noticed how some people seem superhuman when it comes to getting things done? They finish projects early at work, coach their kids' soccer team, volunteer on the weekend, go to the gym regularly, and somehow still have time to get plenty of sleep. It's hard not to be in awe of these people—and even harder not to be envious.

We all have the same number of hours in the day, and yet it translates into totally different results. Of course, some of this is related to drive. The people who set out to accomplish more will surpass those who don't take initiative. But it goes beyond that. Many people desire to achieve great things but can't seem to find the time in their schedule. Instead of getting ahead, they feel like they're just trying to keep up. At work, there's a seemingly endless barrage of emails and nonessential meetings, along with tedious tasks that take up way too much time. At home, the laundry piles up, the dog is putting on extra weight because he doesn't get enough exercise, and the fridge never seems to hold options that form a coherent meal. Just getting through the week is a battle, and by the time Friday rolls around, rest and relaxation sound more appealing than anything productive. We've all been there—whether it's lasted for a few weeks or become the new normal.

Constantly struggling to keep your head above water is a soul-crushing experience that you do not have to endure. No matter your goals, it's essential to gain control of your daily schedule so you have time to think, rest, and focus on what really matters. Becoming more efficient can feel like the equivalent of adding hours to your day. As you focus on your personal and career growth, having this extra time is the foundation you need for making real progress.

SYSTEMS

People don't realize how important systems are until they desperately need them. As a leader, you oversee numerous processes, people, and tasks. Chances are there many redundant aspects of your job. Whenever there's a task you plan on performing multiple times, you'll likely benefit from taking the time to develop a system that allows you to do it faster. Systems can include checklists, email templates, or even step-by-step guides for getting things done right.

Think about fast-food restaurants. They have locations all across the country, and yet each time you walk in to order a meal, you know exactly what to expect. Your favorite burger will taste exactly the same in Wisconsin or Texas because it's cooked in a uniform process using the same ingredients. It doesn't matter if it was made by an employee who has been there for 20 years or a high schooler hired last week. Those are systems at their finest.

There are a few key reasons why systems development is a game-changer. First, it can take a lot of time and mental energy to figure out how to do something—and almost just as much time to think through it again later if you forget what you did. Details have a way of getting fuzzy over time, and even if you think you'll remember all the steps, it'll be easier to just write them down.

Clearly recorded systems also make it possible to delegate tasks without much training. One of your colleagues can pick up right where you left off and not miss a beat. This is especially helpful to prevent the trap of needing help but being too busy to train someone on what to do.

If you feel a lack of time is holding you back, you need systems! Systems are essential for growth because they save so much precious time. Eventually, you reach a point where there are simply not enough hours in the day. It takes effort to find the most efficient way to complete various tasks and record the methods so the process is easily replicable—but it pays off.

One of my friends founded a marketing consultancy about 10 years ago, and it wasn't until last year that she realized how much her lack of systems was holding her back. For several years, she did the vast majority of client work, with some help from a few independent contractors. As her business grew and she started bringing in more clients and hiring new freelancers, things started getting hairy. Her team members summitted their hours in different formats and at random times of the month, and clients were invoiced on their own schedules as well. As the company grew, it became incredibly time consuming just to figure out how much work had been done and correctly bill clients for it. She was completely overextended, spending way too much time on tasks that should have been done quicker—and could have easily been delegated to someone else.

Ultimately, she hired a business manager and accountant who completely systemized the business. They introduced QuickBooks, and her contractors started using it to track hours. The system automatically adds the work to invoices, making it easier to run payroll and bill clients. But that's only the tip of the iceberg. Virtually everything about the business became more efficient than ever, from following up with leads to hiring new contractors to filing taxes. It was a painstaking process to overhaul so many unproductive ways of getting things done, but within a few months, my friend found herself with more time to focus on what she does best: working directly with clients. That year, she doubled her revenue. And more importantly, she rekindled her love for owning her business.

Systems don't sound sexy, so most people aren't drawn to them. But they can make a huge impact on your day-to-day reality! Systems save you from tedious, unenjoyable tasks that waste mental energy, allowing you to focus on the work you find most fulfilling.

TYPES OF SYSTEMS

- **Checklists:** Don't underestimate an old-fashioned checklist. Whenever you have multiple tasks, a list helps make sure you don't miss anything.
- **Processes documentation:** If tasks need to be done a certain way, get it on paper so someone else can easily replicate the process.
- **Email templates:** Instead of writing similar emails over and over, come up with a single reusable template that can be easily tailored when necessary.
- **Check-in meetings:** Short, weekly meetings with colleagues or clients can become a great system for tackling non-urgent questions and updates. This alone can significantly reduce the number of emails you send and receive each day.
- **FAQs:** Do you feel like you're answering the same questions from your colleagues over and over? Create an internal FAQ doc for your department. For example, if someone has an IT

question, they should consult the IT FAQs before emailing that department for help.

- **Email folders:** One of the fastest ways to track certain types of information is by filing it into new email folders. For example, if you get or give performance reviews, it's usually time consuming to reflect on everything that's happened since the last one. An easy way to stay organized throughout the year is to create an email folder that's dedicated to performance reviews. When you receive positive feedback from your boss or clients, save it to that folder so you can easily reference it later. If one of your reports does something great (or something not so great), save it to that folder as well. Don't forget that you can always BCC yourself on emails to get a copy of your sent message in your inbox so it can be added to the appropriate folder.
- **Cloud storage:** Utilizing cloud-based storage systems such as Dropbox or Google Drive makes it easier to organize and keep all your data accessible to everyone in your organization so you can be efficient, be productive, and have key documents at your fingertips.

LEVERAGING ONLINE PLATFORMS AND SOFTWARE

Chances are that an online tool has already been created to solve whatever kind of efficiency issue you're facing. Many of these tools have different membership levels, which allows you to access certain features for free.

- **Scheduling:** *Calendly* or *Doodle* can make it so you never have to spend time going back and forth about availability to get a call on the calendar. You just send people a link to book time with you and the tool automatically populates your availability and sends a calendar invitation.

- **Project management:** *Asana, Slack,* and *Monday.com* can track your team's deliverables, update you on progress, and keep deadlines front and center. Instead of having to send emails and check in with multiple people, you assign projects and send notes in the system.

- **Time tracking:** *Harvest* and *Toggl* make it easy to clock in and out for hourly work. At the end of the month, you can export your time sheet and the total amount you are owed per project will populate on your invoice.

- **Accounting:** *QuickBooks* and *FreshBooks* make bookkeeping easy and give you valuable data on income and expenses throughout the year. You also can accept payments through the system so you don't have to worry about cashing checks and recording that they were received.

- **Social media:** *Hootsuite* and *Loomly* help streamline your outreach and track engagement on multiple platforms. With all your data in one spot, it's quick and easy to analyze results.

- **Audio, video, and screen recording:** *Loom* and *BombBomb* enable you to send messages faster than writing emails or having live meetings. They can be a great option for creating personalized how-to videos that people can bookmark to watch again later.

- **Customer-relationship management (CRM):** *Salesforce, Insightly,* and *Zoho* can help track leads, sales, and every customer interaction. These kinds of tools enable all kinds of things, from automatically sending follow-up emails at certain points in a customer journey to tracking your team's sales performance.

Many of these tools have overlapping functionalities. Do your research before choosing a solution to make sure you get one that's the right fit for your overall needs.

I've learned a good chunk of what I know about systems from Chris Penasa. Chris is the CEO of Small Business Growth Partners (SBGP), a consulting firm that specializes in the trade industry. Chris and I met years ago, and he's become a mentor to me. His thriving business focuses on helping clients create systems that drive growth, so it's no surprise that SBGP runs like a well-oiled machine.

One of the most impressive systems that Chris created is the one that tells him exactly when he needs to hire a new employee, and for what role. He invested the time up front figuring out profit and cashflow triggers, so he always knows his next three hires. He also created an organizational chart with clear roles and responsibilities for each position, so there is no question about expectations. This makes hiring and accountability a breeze.

"Create systems that get you out of the firing line," Chris advised. "Start with the things you do the most often and then the things you dislike doing the most."

EXERCISE: GET SYSTEMATIZED!

Come up with three operations that you can improve by developing new systems. Set a deadline for each one and get to work!

Many systems arise from trial and error. When something starts getting out of hand, people realize they need a system. This can work, but it's better to be proactive about your systems before certain processes start draining time and energy. When you do something for the first time, consider the likelihood that you'll end up doing it again. If likely, create a system! Future you will thank you.

TIME MANAGEMENT

No one sets out to intentionally waste time. We don't wake up in the morning and think, "How can I let the day totally get away from me so I'm constantly busy but never manage to finish what's most important?" And yet this is the reality we sometimes find ourselves in.

Systems go a long way toward saving time, but to become more efficient, you need to manage your schedule. The key is to go from reactive to proactive scheduling. When you're reactive with time management, you plod along, responding to things as they come up. You answer emails as they come in, you schedule meetings whenever people request them, and you generally don't keep your eye on the clock. This can be great for serving other people, but it's easy to find yourself constantly playing catchup without enough time left to accomplish your most pressing tasks. As you advance in your career and your responsibilities increase, the list of people who want something from you is only going to grow.

For children, one of the easiest words to say is "no." Children are self-centered by nature, and they act in their own interests. As adults, we become people pleasers. We want to be liked—for good reason! Likeability absolutely matters when it comes to getting ahead at work. But in our effort to be seen as helpful, cooperative, and empathetic, we often compromise our time and our own self-interests.

If you're striving for exponential career growth, you need to start viewing your time as your most precious commodity. Protect it at all costs. If something isn't worthy of your time, figure out how to tactfully turn it down. Say things like, "Thank you so much for thinking of me for this opportunity. Unfortunately, I just don't have the bandwidth to commit to it at this time, but I might be able to recommend someone else you could ask."

You also need to beware of letting monkeys pile up on your back. This is a metaphor for letting others unload their burdens onto you. Whenever you find yourself tasked with something that is not central to reaching your main goals, you have a monkey on your back. Monkeys have a way of accumulating and weighing you down so your inclination is to deal with them one by one in order to move on to what really matters. But sometimes hours can go by while you answer emails and do the work to remove the monkeys, only to find they just keep coming back. This is a classic productivity problem, and it's the kind of thing that can escalate and turn into a much larger issue. If you feel like you're constantly going out of your way to help other people do their jobs—at the expense of your own—it can make you resentful and bitter. Don't let it get to that point.

No matter your job, it is not your responsibility to solve everyone else's problems. Even if you want to be helpful, be resourceful, and show your worth at your organization, doing whatever anyone asks of you is not a good use of time. Constantly putting out other people's fires is neither satisfying nor rewarding. It wears you down and steals your energy, keeping you from doing the deep thinking and hard work necessary to improve your business and enjoy life.

The key to keeping monkeys off your back is empowering people to answer their own questions. Let's say that a direct report forwards you a tough question from a client and asks how you want to respond. That takes the monkey off their back and puts it on yours. Now you're tasked with reviewing the email, thinking through options for responding, and typing up an appropriate reply. Instead of accepting that monkey, you should reply to your direct report and ask, "What do you recommend?" This forces them to take responsibility for the work while still affording you an opportunity to weigh in on the answer.

Depending on your company culture, there may be a need to train others on ways to avoid transferring their monkeys to other people's backs. I advise my team to come to me with a problem only after they're ready to also present a potential solution. This not only saves me the time of having to solve simple issues, but it empowers team members to come up with new, innovative ideas for improvements. Rather than thinking they need to defer to me to solve every issue, they can learn to apply their own skills while still providing me a chance to check their work and give feedback. In turn, this boosts self-esteem and reinforces the confidence necessary for them to tackle more difficult issues in the future.

If you have a colleague who habitually puts monkeys on your back, a good trick to get them to change their behavior is to always ask for something in return. Say something like, "I'll help you figure this out, but in return I need your help with XYZ." If you do that a couple of times, you'll see how quickly your colleague can solve problems on their own.

Another smart solution for staying dialed in to your top priorities is scheduling time for it in your calendar. I call this a "default calendar." I always try to pre-schedule time to work on my bigger projects, especially during a time of day when I feel I am most focused or have the most energy. For me, it's right away in the morning or after lunch.

If you have an empty calendar, your brain automatically equates that with having free time—even if you're under deadline. If you block the majority of your workday for specific projects, you'll be less likely to agree to unproductive meetings or find yourself surfing the internet instead of focusing on your goals.

I like to block my calendar with recurring sessions for ongoing tasks, and before I leave the office on Friday, I take a close look at the week ahead just to make sure I have everything planned out. Creating a simple to-do list on Friday afternoon frees up my mind for the weekend. That way, when I come in on Monday morning, I'm sufficiently rested and know exactly what I need to work on that whole week.

Discipline is the key to taking control of your schedule once and for all. When you block off time on your calendar, you need to treat it just as seriously as you would if you were meeting with someone else. Put your phone on silent and resist the urge to check your email. Don't let anything derail your productivity. With discipline, it's amazing how much you can accomplish.

EXERCISE: TIME AUDIT

For the next week, take notes on how you spend your time. (Try using a free time-tracking platform!) Be honest if a chunk of time passes and you aren't quite sure what you did because it wasn't much. At the end of the week, analyze how you spent your time. Was it a good reflection of what's most important to you? If not, home in on the areas that are sucking your time and make a plan for efficiency. Figure out how many extra hours each week you can shift toward things that align with your goals and make you happy. Visit my website to download a free time-tracker sheet at www.davidbelman.net/resources/time.

CUTTING BACK ON CUSTOMIZATION

Customization can drastically compromise efficiency. Whether it's putting together highly personalized quotes or delivering bespoke service packages, you may find yourself spending a great deal of time trying to cater to customers' every whim. The reality is that you can't be everything to everyone. If you can find a way to cut back on customization by creating a few different packages, it can be a great option for unlocking time in your busy schedule.

As a home builder, I'm extremely familiar with customers' desires to personalize. People often think that one of the most exciting parts of buying a new home is picking out the tile, fixtures, and paint colors. In the past, we were very flexible and allowed buyers a ton of opportunities to design their perfect aesthetic. We wanted to continue providing buyers with that experience, but the time it consumed was becoming a pain point in the business. For each customer, we had to explain all the options, give them time to decide on all the details, and then take special care during the building process to follow instructions that were different for every single house. Ultimately, it was too taxing on our team, and the amount of work was driving up our prices.

This year, I decided to try something new. I bought a plot of land that would fit 54 homes and I created packaged options for customers. Instead of offering literally millions of potential combinations, my team and I came up with six interchangeable floor plans, streamlining it to just a handful of decisions on a variety of features. Although we offered fewer choices, the sales message was stronger because it was simple.

We threw a grand opening at the site and invited prospective buyers to see the development area. Because the packages were so simple, customers could quickly make selections from the list of possible options, and we could give them a quote within minutes. We sold six houses that week! That never would have been possible if we hadn't cut back on customization.

A few customers asked about going beyond the packages to personalize their home, but we explained that, because it increases our efficiency, the packages enable us to provide a great price. It's possible that we lost a customer or two because we decided not to honor every request, but we certainly gained more than we lost.

Think about your professional role. Where could you cut back on customization to improve efficiency? Instead of viewing fewer options as a negative, determine how a streamlined process could actually benefit all parties.

Efficiency will dramatically change your daily life. It takes effort to keep organized and develop the right systems, as well as discipline in how you spend your time, but it's worth it. Start small. Make simple changes and go from there. If you improve just a little bit every day, you'll soon be in a completely different spot than where you are today.

CHAPTER 5

PRACTICING INTENTIONAL LEADERSHIP

Dad launched our family business in 1981. It was headquartered in the basement of our home. At the time, the country was in the middle of a recession. (Interest rates were nearly 18%!) Needless to say, my dad took some risks. Early on, he took a chance and purchased some land from some bigger companies in the Milwaukee area that had overextended themselves. He hoped to build new homes on the properties. Because things were slow and not a lot of companies were building, my dad was able to hire some of the most talented tradespeople and put them to work. In the beginning, he spent a lot of time sitting around waiting for the phone to ring, but the economy turned around soon after that and business started taking off.

Unfortunately, my dad was never that great at recruiting. If someone said they needed a job, my dad would hire them. There was no lens for vetting candidates to see if they would be a good fit; there had never been any thought or discussion as to what a "good fit" would even look like. It should come as no surprise that my dad soon found himself surrounded by people who created problems and were generally hard to manage. Some employees had bad attitudes, others had nasty tempers, and quite a few showed up late almost every day—if they came in at all. Over the next decade, the culture (if you could even call it that) continued to spread as the company expanded.

I was just out of high school when we moved the business to an office building and I started working full time. I noticed there was little communication on rules or expectations and absolutely no semblance of order. I didn't have experience at other companies to know what was normal, but one day in particular made me realize we had some serious internal issues.

Jeff, who had worked for one of our competitors, sent in his résumé looking for a job, and my dad interviewed him. A few days later, our core team met in the office for a meeting. My dad was running late. With everyone waiting, Jeff walks right into the conference room, sits down with us at the table, and says, "Good morning." We all just gaped at him, thinking, "What's this guy doing here?" My dad had hired him and never told any of us. To say it was awkward would be an understatement. Fifteen years later, we're lucky to still have Jeff on the team. He laughs about it now, but he said he never felt more unwelcome in his entire life than he did on his first day at our company.

All these years later, thinking about that meeting still makes me cringe. My dad was a great man and always did right by our customers, but his focus was never on internal leadership or company culture. From the very beginning, it was clear this was a key area where we could improve.

Comparing the company then to how it is today is like night and day. This level of change didn't happen by accident; it took intentional, consistent action and hard work. Things started to shift when I led the process to develop our vision statement: *Creating the Ultimate Building Experience One Customer at a Time*. From there, we created our mission statement, which includes strategies on how we deliver on the vision. Lastly, we created our 14 Points of Culture, which are the principles we follow to achieve our goals. I wanted to develop these policies so they could serve as our North Star, guiding everything from long-term planning to our daily frame of mind. In the short term, this also gave our whole team a newfound sense of direction and some much-needed inspiration.

Our "A" players bought into the initiative immediately and took it as a challenge to raise the bar on how we conduct business. This inspired other team members and helped establish a critical mass of support for our newly defined cultural expectations. Although the reaction from the team overall was incredibly positive, there were a few who thought the whole thing was a waste of time. As you probably can guess, those were the people whose actions were never in line with the best interests of the company. As the company evolved, we parted ways with those who weren't supportive of the new direction. Because we had outlined our goals and could assess objectively whether people's actions were aligned with or detracting from them, this was actually fairly easy. This may seem like a small thing, but it's something we had never been able to do before. It enabled us to get the right group of people on board, which kick-started a new level of success.

Almost immediately, we started selling more, the team became happier and more cohesive, and awards and accolades poured in. Today, about half of our staff has been with the company for more than a decade. Although we had chugged along and were doing okay before these efforts, we got so much more successful once I focused on leadership and worked hard to create a positive, uplifting culture.

Sometimes it can seem cheesy when organizations are proactive about shaping their company culture. No one wants to feel like certain beliefs or values are forced upon them just so senior leaders can check a box. With that said, things can go very wrong if you completely ignore culture and let it develop on its own in the wild. When you proactively craft your mission, vision, and values, it sets clear expectations for what matters most to succeed at the organization.

If you work for an organization that has defined its mission, vision, and values, think of these as your cheat sheet for getting ahead. If you've ever wondered how to get noticed and impress your boss and senior leaders, start by embodying the characteristics and actions outlined by the company's specific goals. This might seem like common sense, but it can be easy to overlook, especially if your company doesn't provide ongoing communication or reminders on direction.

As a leader, be aware when team members' actions align with your company values. I tune into it on a daily basis, and it's how I assess performance, individually and overall. In order to align your behaviors with your company's goals, set aside time for a refresher on your company's official statements—especially if you haven't read them since you were given the employee handbook! Write down a few things you could start doing differently to better embody those values and look for actions that will be visible to others and set a good example.

If your company has not yet created any values statements, it might be time to connect with your manager or an HR leader and suggest that the team collaborate to develop some. This will show you're proactive and want to act in the best interest of the company but would benefit from gaining a better understanding on what's most important.

In addition to following your company's mission, vision, and values, you should create your own personal version. The great thing about defining these standards is they provide a clear sense of direction. When you face a difficult situation and you have trouble deciding how to handle it, just cross-reference your options with your personal values statement. Chances are certain behaviors or actions will align better than others.

Creating a vision statement will help you and your team grow immeasurably. The process is fairly easy, but it will take several reviews and revisions to get it right. To create a vision statement for yourself or your company, feel free to use the template below. To print your own copy, visit www.davidbelman.net/resources/culture.

I suggest starting with your vision statement. Think of this as where you want to go. It should be fairly short, preferably one sentence. Your vision statement should push you or your team. It should be inspiring. If it doesn't motivate the heck out of you, keep trying.

Once you have an idea of your vision, start to craft your mission statement. The mission statement should include a few sentences on how you plan to achieve your vision. It should describe who you are, what you do, and why you do it.

The mission statement is a good place to differentiate yourself or your company from competitors. Highlight what you do (or will do) that sets you apart. For a company, what is your unique selling proposition? If it is a personal vision statement, what make you unique? Describe what you are best at.

Next are the points of culture. Think of these as the skills you will need to pull it all off. Ask yourself, "What do I need to get better at to achieve this? What skills do I need to develop?" Make bold statements. Once identified, write a short sentence about how those skills fit into your vision and mission. There is no perfect number of points of culture. You could have three or fifteen. Just remember the more points of culture you have, the harder they are to remember or relay to a team. When in doubt, less is more. You can always add more once you master those skills.

As you prepare this, you may have to go back and forth between your vision, mission, and culture a few times to get it just right. Don't worry—this is perfectly normal. Working on it, reviewing it, and coming back to it later will help make a better document. If this is a company mission statement, engage your team in the process. They will likely have some great insights into reaching your potential. Engaging your team also helps create buy-in and support for your vision.

After you finish this exercise, make it a habit to look back at this process. Review it in team meetings. You will know it is working when your team is confronted with a choice and asks, "Is this decision consistant with our culture?" Or they come to you and say, "I don't think this aligns with who we are." If this happens, just smile and know that you have created a winning culture.

Creating a Vision, Mission, and Culture

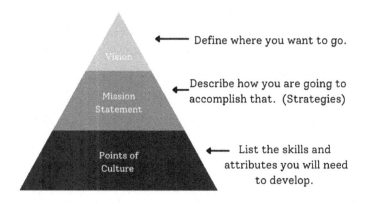

Vision — Define where you want to go.

Mission Statement — Describe how you are going to accomplish that. (Strategies)

Points of Culture — List the skills and attributes you will need to develop.

As you familiarize yourself with the process of weighing your choices against your values, your actions will become more intentional. Instead of being guided by short-lived emotions, your actions will represent the person you truly want to be. This is the hallmark of great leadership.

As you reflect on becoming an intentional leader, here are a few areas to keep in mind:

- **Consistency:** Reliability will suit you well no matter your role or industry. When people know they can count on you to follow through, you'll be given even more responsibilities—and opportunities. This is how you build your reputation and make a name for yourself.
- **Accountability:** A good leader rarely takes credit, but they step up quickly to take blame. It's hard to admit when you're wrong, but that's how you earn respect. (And the bigger the screwup, the more accountability matters!) You might be surprised how far a simple apology can go, both with colleagues and customers. Oftentimes, accountability is all it takes to make a situation right. If you can be vulnerable and admit fault, people will think more of you—despite your mistake.
- **Empowerment:** When you let go, you give people the opportunity to shine. They might not do everything exactly as you would, but resist the urge to micromanage their projects. It will only suck up time and frustrate your colleagues. (This is an area where I used to struggle. I practiced my mantra, "I am a great delegator," and it served as a helpful reminder to have faith in my team to get the job done.)
- **Responsibility:** Sometimes you'll sense a problem brewing in the workplace but it seems easier to turn a blind eye than to proactively deal with it. If you choose to go along as normal

and pretend everything is fine, you'll only feed the problem, giving it extra time to grow. This is often the case when an employee no longer seems to be a good fit at the company. Firing and hiring can be so much work, but delaying the inevitable only makes it worse. Intentional leaders avoid denial and make tough decisions quickly, just like ripping off a bandage. The old adage is to hire slowly but fire quickly, and that advice will stand the test of time. At my organization, we are deliberate about hiring people, and they must pass a thorough vetting before we bring them on the team.

- **Trustworthiness:** The best relationships are built on trust. When colleagues and clients have faith in you, it opens doors for a tremendous amount of growth. But unfortunately, all of that trust can be lost in an instant if you make a bad decision and don't own up. Stupid mistakes can be forgiven quickly, but compromising your integrity is different. To avoid breaking trust, just do the right thing—even when no one is looking.

- **Recognition:** Many employee engagement studies have shown that recognition for a job well done is key for fulfillment at work. In other words, people want to know that they—and their work—are appreciated. That's why it's so important to call out wins, recognize colleagues for going above and beyond, and celebrate success. At Belman Homes, we have a peer award every month called "The Top Dawg." Recipients are nominated by their teammates, and the nominations are read out loud in the monthly meeting—so everyone gets to hear the nice things people said about them and the whole team stays in the loop on their colleagues' achievements. We also have celebrations whenever our company wins an award. Our team members vote on a few different options, like renting a boat or going out to a nice dinner, and we take the time to celebrate together.

WHAT IF YOU DON'T MANAGE A TEAM?

A leader is someone that others follow. Your followers don't need to appear beneath you in an organizational chart. And on the flip side, just because people report to you doesn't mean that you're a true leader. We all look to others for inspiration and guidance—often without even realizing it. We see what works for others and instinctually try to tap into that for our own growth. Sometimes we're inspired by colleagues, industry leaders, celebrities, and even those younger than us who have less experience. Leadership is about actions and outlook, not titles.

Get to know your colleagues. Find out what's important to them and how you might be able to help. Part of being a leader means caring about others and going out of your way to serve them.

POLITICS

We would be missing a major piece of the growth-hacking puzzle if we failed to address politics. In other words, navigating the oh-so-pleasant world of petty grievances, inflated egos, and the repercussions of accidentally (or intentionally) stepping on one another's toes. In every organization, politics is an undercurrent that constantly affects the flow of work. It's the reason why certain people and projects find quick success while others get bottlenecked and never move forward. This intangible force can be with you, against you, or pass you by. To get ahead at your organization, you need to understand the politics at play.

You're probably familiar with your company's organizational chart, but this structure does not mirror the power dynamics. A senior leader might wield very little influence, whereas someone further down has more power than you would expect. For example, a VP might defer to her administrative assistant's opinion on a wide range of topics, from selecting vendors and prioritizing meetings to drafting department policies and hiring key staff. Some people in the company who have gotten to know this VP and/or her assistant are sure to understand the politics: to get the VP on your side, you have to win over her assistant. But what about everyone else? Those who don't understand the politics would tailor their emails, sales presentations, and other correspondences with the VP in mind, not knowing that she might never even review their work.

As you think about advancing your career, keep this kind of interpersonal dynamic top of mind. It's possible that there are hidden stakeholders you haven't considered, whether it's within your own company, in a volunteer role, or for a client you are trying to win over.

A few years ago, I became president of the Metropolitan Builders Association. I was excited to have the role and eager to drive some changes I thought would improve the organization. I took it slow for the first several months as I got a feel for the politics and stakeholders. When I thought I understood everything at play, I tried to change some of the association's bylaws that I felt were holding us back. I wanted to modify how board members were selected, the criteria for becoming a leader of the association, and the cadence of certain meetings. They had the same meeting three times in one week just for different stakeholders! I spoke with a lot of our members, and everyone seemed to be in favor of the changes.

Though it looked promising at first, I soon realized I had failed to consider one important group calling shots behind the scenes: past leaders of the association. It didn't occur to me that if I made changes after those influencers no longer held leadership roles, it might impact their legacies. If I changed a policy that they chose to uphold and it made things better, it could undercut their past accomplishments.

And on the flip side, if one of my changes made something worse, it would damage the quality of the association they had worked so hard at improving. In terms of driving major change, I realized it was a "damned if you do, damned if you don't" situation.

In the end, the pushback proved to be too much. Members who originally aligned with my proposals didn't want to break allegiances with past leaders, to whom they ultimately deferred for their vote. Despite this, the organization adopted about half of my proposed changes, and they are now considering more of them. They weren't bad ideas; it was just too much change too quickly for some folks.

When working with a large group, there will always be different factions who have specific interests. People have sacred cows they will protect at all costs, whether those things are truly serving them or not. It's helpful to be aware of those dynamics before taking a path that might not lead anywhere good.

Focus on small changes to manage politics while still trying to get noticed. Figure out how to fix minor issues that are obviously not serving the organization. Take time to structure an unorganized process or volunteer to improve something that benefits a specific department. As you stack up successes, you'll gain trust and respect from your colleagues, as well as influence. Little by little, this adds up. This kind of intentionality is exactly what will propel your career forward.

DAVID BELMAN
LEADERSHIP GROWTH HACKS

VISION STATEMENT

VISION:

_____

MISSION STATEMENT:

_____

POINTS OF CULTURE:

CHAPTER 6

DEVELOPING YOUR PERSONAL BRAND

A personal brand is all about helping people get to know and like you—in as little time as possible. Likability will earn you more opportunities in life than any other factor—including experience. People simply do business with people they like. Whether it's choosing a new CPA, picking which coffee shop to go to, or making the final decision after interviewing three job candidates, we all make decisions based on how others make us feel. That's why it's smart to be proactive about managing your personal brand.

It's easy to see why we should all want to craft an image that helps others see us in a positive light, but the tricky part is understanding what that looks like and how to do it. Certain qualities are universally admirable, such as trustworthiness, knowledge, and honesty. But beyond that, leaders often aren't sure of other qualities to show off.

By developing your personal brand, you are choosing to show

more of yourself to the world. Let your guard down so that the real you can shine through and show who you really are and what you stand for. Without this level of openness, though you might not be presenting a negative perception of yourself, you certainly aren't putting forth a positive one either. Though you may feel as though you are safe-guarding yourself from negative perceptions, you're making yourself totally forgettable. This will not serve you well when it comes time for a promotion or getting a referral to your ideal client.

People are afraid to put themselves out there and be in the spotlight because they are afraid of what others will think. If you post about your accomplishments on social media, will people think you're a narcissist? Or if you let down your walls and try to get to know your colleagues at work, will they choose not to reciprocate?

Due to the COVID-19 pandemic, the number of those working from home increased, and the line between work and life has blurred. We've been taught to be professional in the workplace, to maintain composure and treat others with the same respect and decorum we expect for ourselves. Suddenly, we find ourselves Zoomed into our colleagues' and clients' bedrooms while their kids scream at each other in some (not-so) distant corner of the house. All of the norms and long-time standards have shifted for what it means to be a professional, and we only can expect this trend to continue. It's no wonder that people feel unsure of how much of themselves to show in the workplace and how that translates to social platforms that colleagues and clients might see.

The LinkedIn networking platform is usually crowded with buttoned-up, dry posts, which is why Shay Rowbottom's appearances in my feed caught my eye. She was always delivering informative content in a funny and engaging way. Compared with the rest of my LinkedIn connections, Shay seemed raw and uncensored. This approach has proven incredibly successful in building her digital marketing consultancy. With only a few years' experience in marketing and no formal education in business, she has made a name for herself advising high-profile CEOs on how they can develop their personal brands online.

Shay told me that she got her start when she was at her breaking point. Frustrated and fed up with her job and the professional world in general, she shot a video of herself venting—and it got a massive response online. She was shocked at how well a little authenticity cut through all the noise. That's when she realized it was okay to be herself.

"It happened by accident," Shay said. "I had anxiety and depression. I was in a bad place and I just started sharing and venting, and it liberated me. I saw the response that people had to the content, and it resonated with them. In a way, it gave permission to others to be vulnerable."

Rather than trying to please everyone with bland, milquetoast posts, Shay gained traction for her authenticity. This approach helped catch the attention of business guru Grant Cardone, and the two formed an unlikely friendship. Shay learned that her brand wasn't for everyone, but it helped her connect with the people who really mattered for growing her business. According to Shay, "In order to find your best clients, you have to be willing to put up with and move past the people who dislike you."

As you think about developing your own personal brand, authenticity is key. Be yourself. You are unique, and by showcasing the qualities that define who you are—both in person and online—you will cultivate a personal brand that's relatable and memorable.

A great way to display your individuality is through the lens of your passions. Where do you get your energy and enthusiasm? Think about your industry and professional role, but don't forget your personal life. Maybe you love ballroom dancing, or riding rollercoasters, or bad horror movies form the '80s—whatever makes you light up when you talk about it. Your enthusiasm will be infectious. Tap into your passions to bring your true self front and center.

Be proactive about putting yourself out there. Sharing what's going on in your world gives others an opportunity to get to know you better. Maybe it's posting more photos on social media, writing an industry-related blog, or creating a YouTube channel. These efforts can feel scary at first, but they make a big difference in showing who you are and what you're all about.

To resonate with your audience and not sound "salesy" or braggadocious, focus on helpful information. On a regular basis, try to proactively answer questions that your clients might have. Start conversations that delve into topics that matter to them and provide insight not available elsewhere.

Most of my competitors aren't very active on social media. They simply don't prioritize online branding. I saw this as a huge opportunity to gain an advantage as the owner of a home-development company. I wanted to become known as the top builder in the Milwaukee area, so I focused on cultivating the right personal brand, both for Belman Homes and for myself. I started a home-building podcast called *The Home Building Hero*, and I became active on LinkedIn and Twitter. My competitors thought it was a bit strange—and they let me know it! On several occasions, using a tone of voice that conveyed more skepticism than approval, they've said something like, "You sure are on social media a lot."

They probably thought I was wasting my time, especially in the beginning. Initially, it was difficult connecting directly with home buyers. My customers weren't on Twitter looking for home-building advice, but I kept posting informative content. After a while, I started gaining the attention of reporters writing stories about the housing market. I was quoted as a home-building expert in a variety of articles, which helped me connect with a wider audience.

Shaping my personal brand made a world of difference in my organization's success. Home buyers can get a good feel for who we are and what we're all about just by Googling us. And the best part is that they don't have to rely on what we're saying on our website—they can see what other people are saying about us. When we meet with new clients, they often talk about how they saw us on TV giving away a free home to a veteran, or how they read about us in an article. That goes a long way in helping prospective clients get to know and like us.

It won't always be smooth sailing (I should know!), but you have to ride out the highs and lows. Not everything I publish gets high engagement, and that's okay. When the COVID pandemic first hit the U.S., everyone's priorities shifted. And despite listenership dropping 30%, I kept recording podcasts. While other podcasters went silent, I put time and effort into releasing three episodes a week, right on schedule. It was important to me to stay relevant and continue connecting with my network, even if they were distracted. A few months later, listenership spiked as people came back to the podcast and listened to episodes they had missed.

I've spoken with other leaders and entrepreneurs who had similar experiences. When things got slow, they used the extra time to invest in building their personal brands. They continued showing up for their audiences and staying top of mind even when engagement dipped, and now they're busier than ever. It's been a good lesson in the power of momentum. Once you get moving, the worst thing you can do is pump the breaks.

BUILD THE RIGHT NETWORK

Have you ever heard the saying "it's not about what you know; it's about who you know"? It might not be fair, but the reality is that connections can open doors leading anywhere you want to go in life. That's why you should make the conscious effort to get to know the right kinds of people. I'm not suggesting you identify the 10 most powerful people in your industry and go on a quest to butter them up. But I am saying that you need to surround yourself with people who have similar goals, interests, and personal brands.

You reflect what you take in. If you align yourself with positive, productive people who have a growth mindset, they will provide positive reinforcement and challenge you to up your game. This also positions you for introductions and referrals. When people have worked hard to cultivate a positive reputation, it means a lot when they recommend you to their network. Whether you're trying to secure a sales meeting, a job interview, or anything between, these kinds of introductions are a huge advantage.

Get to know the people in your industry as well as those who provide a different product or service for the same target market. For example, if you're a freelance graphic designer who works with small businesses, it would be helpful to network with other professionals who share your clients, such as photographers, writers, website developers, and administrative specialists. Any of them could be an excellent source of referrals. A strong personal brand can in turn position you as the "go-to" person whenever anyone in your network has a client who needs a graphic designer.

If you work for an organization, make an effort to build stronger relationships with colleagues and senior leaders. Become known as someone who is helpful, motivated, and making an impact. We'll talk more about exactly how to do that in the next chapter, but it's important to know that getting the right people on your side can shape your personal brand and provide access to even greater opportunities.

It can be jaw-dropping to look back and see how a series of events all stemmed from one relationship. Whenever I feel like I'm too busy to keep up with LinkedIn, I remind myself of the power that just one new connection can have. For example, if I hadn't gotten involved in Operation Finally Home and posted about it on social media, I never would have met my friend Paul M. Neuberger. That means we wouldn't have partnered to found The Young Guns Movement, an organization for growth-minded entrepreneurs and leaders. Through YG, I've made dozens of new connections. The butterfly effect of just one social-media post altered the course of my life and business.

STORYTELLING

Knowing what to say is challenging when starting conversations—especially online. What should you talk about? What will people care about?

The biggest influencers on social media are talented storytellers. Their content is interesting and engaging. Are these influencers different than the rest of us? Does life magically serve them up likeable, share-worthy content every single day from the moment they hop out of bed? No way! Influencers get to where they are in part because of their ability to turn lemons into lemonade.

We all have stories that could put an audience on the edges of their seats. The challenge is recognizing the raw material that creates such stories and packaging it in a way that is accessible and supports your personal brand. When you learn to craft interesting stories from everyday life, you will gain a huge advantage in shaping your image because you'll never be at a loss for words.

Great storytelling takes practice, but focusing on the elements below will help. Your life is filled with material—it's just a matter of recognizing it.

ELEMENTS OF GOOD STORYTELLING

- **Authenticity:** The most interesting stories won't paint a perfect picture of you or your life. In fact, they might show the opposite—your humbling moments, mistakes, or challenges. If a story leaves you feeling vulnerable, you're probably tapping into something worth telling. Give people a peek behind the veil. When you are authentic and share the good and bad in your life, your imperfections will make you even more likeable.

- **Emotion:** The element of any story that draws people in is the emotion. Whether it's joy, pain, humor, embarrassment, or anything between, if a moment in your life made you feel something deeply, chances are that it could make a great story.

- **"So what?":** This often is the hardest part of retelling your story. Why should people care? Some stories have a clear resolution or teachable moment, but not everything can be wrapped up with a pretty bow at the end. Some experiences call for us to reflect on what happened and draw our own conclusions.

- **Tie to personal brand:** Mine stories from your personal life in addition to the work you do to demonstrate the values of your personal brand. For example, moments that show your integrity, resilience, or compassion are relevant because they show who you are as a person.

- **Imagery:** In the digital age, visuals help catch people's attention. Photos don't have to be perfect. In fact, posting too many over-filtered images can detract from your authenticity. The biggest thing is to remember to take photos or videos whenever you're doing something interesting. Another great option is to shoot a video of yourself telling a story.

REMOTE BRANDING

As more work is done from home, it might be time to overhaul how you show up for video meetings. People you've known awhile can overlook bad lighting and a messy home office, but first impressions still matter—as do second and third impressions. If you want to be seen as a knowledgeable professional more than capable of getting the job done, you'll need to step up your game.

- **Camera:** If you have an older computer, it might be worth buying an external camera that will record a clearer picture.
- **Audio:** Your cellphone or your computer's built-in microphone are probably fine for video meetings, but an external mic will do a much better job of cutting background noise when recording content.
- **Lighting:** This is probably the hardest thing to master, but it makes the biggest difference when you get it right. As you probably already know, having a window behind you does not look good on camera, and relying on lights you already own will likely give you subpar results. Your best option is to buy a small, inexpensive light that sits on your desk or attaches to your monitor or laptop. Ideally, you want to be able to adjust the brightness and choose between bright white or a warmer color.
- **Background:** Even if you're limited to your home-office setup, try to have a background that isn't too busy or too plain. If you have a laptop, turn on the camera and walk around your home to test out different areas. You might find an unexpected nook perfect for video meetings.
- **Script:** It helps to have your key talking points written down so your video remains focused and on point. You can use a whiteboard or larger printed notes to help keep you on track.

Don't be afraid to hire someone if you don't understand or enjoy parts of video production. You can inexpensively hire someone to clean your audio or edit your videos. They will do it faster and more efficiently so you can focus on producing good content. This also will help you "scale up" your operation. After all, leadership is all about delegating.

Don't let your desire for perfection stop you from producing content. Practice makes perfect. Your later videos will be light years better than your first ones. In no time, you will be creating engaging content to help you become a trusted name in your industry.

EXERCISE

What are three things you could do this week to impact your personal brand? Block some time in your calendar to get them done.

Managing your image is an ongoing project that will become easier with practice. It's okay to take baby steps. Here is a list of ideas to get you started.

— *Update your social-media profiles with new photos.*
— *Connect with or follow people in your industry.*
— *Write an article or blog post that ties to one of your passions.*
— *Shoot a video that answers a common question from your clients.*
— *Tell people what gets you out of bed in the morning and what excites you about your industry.*
— *Reconnect with an old contact.*
— *Register for a networking event.*
— *Pull out your collection of business cards and send them connection requests.*
— *Don't just be a lurker. If a post made you think, respond to the author and let them know.*

- *Anytime you are doing something new, something different, or something that excites you, share it!*
- *If you are spending too much time thinking about what to post, make yourself a content calendar. Brainstorm a list of ideas and then assign them days to create an easy guide.*
- *Develop a brand anchor. This is something that people remember you by. It could be a hashtag, an emoji, or a pin you always wear.*
- *Strike up a conversation with a stranger on social media.*
- *Buy new equipment for video meetings.*

Lastly, understand that consistency is key. Many people get all excited and make a few videos or podcasts. They don't get the instant gratification of a large number of views and give up too early. I host a leading podcast on construction called The Home Building Hero. It has surpassed many others of its kind because I consistently publish several times a week so my audience knows they can count on new information coming out timely.

DAVID BELMAN
LEADERSHIP GROWTH HACKS

PERSONAL BRAND
CHECKLIST

YEARLY

- [ ] _____
- [ ] _____
- [ ] _____
- [ ] _____

MONTHLY

- [ ] _____
- [ ] _____
- [ ] _____
- [ ] _____

WEEKLY

- [ ] _____
- [ ] _____
- [ ] _____
- [ ] _____
- [ ] _____

PERSONAL BRAND
CHECKLIST

DAVID BELMAN
LEADERSHIP GROWTH HACKS

YEARLY

- [ ] Update your profile picture, bio, and awards
- [ ] Make a list of social media goals for the year
- [ ] Review your performance on platforms and determine the best areas to focus on
- [ ] Create a master content brainstorm list

MONTHLY

- [ ] Create your monthly content calendar
- [ ] Create a blog article
- [ ] Create 1 video
- [ ] Make an email blast

WEEKLY

- [ ] Connect with any new contacts on social media
- [ ] Comment and engage with people's posts
- [ ] Share what you are working on
- [ ] Give some advice on a topic you are knowledgeable on
- [ ] Give someone kudos, then ask to return the favor

CHAPTER 7

UNDERSTANDING VALUE

I once hired a new salesperson who had worked for one of our competitors. She was accustomed to selling homes much cheaper than ours, and she equated value to competitive pricing. When she was about to close her first deal for our company, she came and asked me to speak with the buyer. She said another builder had offered them $15,000 off the price of a similar home, and she was scared of losing the sale. Our company focuses on delivering a quality product rather than bargain pricing, which is a compelling value proposition for many customers—as long as the message is delivered properly.

The buyers pulled up to our meeting, and I took a moment to notice a few things about them before we sat down. First, they drove to our office in a nice new BMW, and when they walked inside, I noticed the wife had a designer handbag. I knew right away they were not going to buy a generic home and price was not their main concern regarding value.

After we said hello and spent a few minutes on small talk, I got right down to business: "I am going to tell you right now that we are not the cheapest builder in town." My salesperson's jaw hit the floor. She thought I had just cost her the sale, and she was kicking herself for bringing me into the process. But then I explained why our houses are more expensive than our competitors'—and that comes down to quality. I explained how we only work with top-level tradespeople and how particular we are about the construction of our homes.

Then I asked how they thought the other builder was able to cut $15,000 from their price, especially considering there were only a few places to go in the area for materials. They guessed the company would try to hire the cheapest labor they could find. "Would you want just anyone working on your home?" I asked them. "Would you want to hire the guy who's $12 cheaper per hour than everyone else?" Of course they wouldn't. This was their home, and it was important to them that the job was done well.

Next, I gently walked them through several things that set our company apart. I explained how other builders may be cheaper, but nobody offers a better total package. They grabbed a pen and signed on the spot. My salesperson was amazed! The price objection she had faced for weeks was over in minutes.

Sometimes people confuse value and pricing. They assume that lower prices equate to higher value. This misconception is understandable considering it's the sales message typically used to market lower-priced goods and services. You don't order a "quality meal" at a fast-food chain; you order a "value meal." But just because something costs less doesn't mean it's innately more valuable than something that costs more, or vice versa. Value is in the eye of the beholder. A good value proposition elicits an emotional response.

It's also important to note that, like price, perceived value does not always align with the amount of effort that went into creating it.

You can work your butt off putting together a 20-page report for your boss, and she might only spend a couple minutes skimming through it because she only cares about one short section. Or you might take two minutes to email your boss about a potential problem with your company's supply chain and that single tip ends up being the most helpful thing you've done since you started working there.

Real value is all about giving people exactly what they want—even if they haven't explicitly told you. Is that tricky? Sometimes. But it's certainly not impossible, and there are plenty of clever ways to understand what people care about most.

Paul M. Neuberger is a serial entrepreneur, sales trainer, author, and close friend. He's also an expert in providing value. He specializes in something most people abhor: cold calling. Paul doesn't call up strangers and ask them to buy; he calls to give. Paul has found that by providing value, he's able to form relationships with new people and widen his personal and professional networks.

He spent a long time thinking about the kinds of products and/or services, anything of value, that he could easily offer to potential customers, and he came up with a few that have resonated especially well. One example is offering to recommend prospects to his network and provide referrals. If he can be a resource to his customers through his insurance agency, and if he is able to provide recommendations to professionals they can trust, such as lawyers, realtors, or interior-design companies, it's an added value. This is how Paul has been able to grow his network exponentially over the years. At the time of writing this book, he has about 30k LinkedIn connections, and I'm sure his network will only grow larger.

Paul says that to provide value, you have to genuinely care about people. With a "give first" mentality, you stop worrying about what's in it for you. Instead of calculating how much you've done versus what others have done in return, focus on helping. When you're invested in other people, you earn their trust and they are more likely to ask what they can do for you in return. It doesn't always happen, and that's fine, but more often than not, people want to reciprocate. New connections routinely introduce Paul to their friends and family, share his social-media posts to help him spread the word about his business, and invite him to their company golf outings and networking events. By providing value to others, it comes back to him in spades.

By going out of your way to help the people you do business with, you will make a real impact that will help take your career to the next level faster than ever before. Here are a few tips for doing just that.

- **Align yourself with your boss's goals:** The best way to provide value for your boss is to focus on the things that matter most to them. Understanding priorities is as simple as asking. Start by saying you want to grab a few minutes with them to make sure you're doing the best possible job you can and you have a few questions. During your meeting, ask your boss about their biggest challenges and whether there is anything you can do to help alleviate any pain points. Ask whether certain projects are a bigger priority than others and how that might change in the future. By having an open, honest conversation and inquiring how you can best be of service, you show initiative and the desire to help. Those two things make a huge difference in demonstrating that you were the right hire and that you're going places quickly.
- **Have an entrepreneurial mindset:** So many working professionals do only what's required of them and go home. They don't go above and beyond because they have no desire to work harder than they have to. Those people do not get

the same opportunities as those who show initiative because colleagues will avoid partnering with them on projects. On the flip side, if you have an entrepreneurial mindset and you're always asking what you can do to make things better, people will be drawn to you because of how much value you are constantly providing. You will make a name for yourself and build a positive reputation because people know they can count on you to go the extra mile. You know you have an entrepreneurial mindset if you find yourself constantly spotting opportunities for improvement as you go about your daily life. When shopping at a store leads you to start evaluating their business model, you know this mindset is one of your strengths!

- **Gain a basic understanding of financials:** Money isn't what's most important, but it does play a role in how decisions are made, both inside a company and when customers make purchases. It helps to have a good understanding of your fixed costs, variable costs, markup, profit margin, and revenue vs. profits. This knowledge will empower you to make better decisions at your company. For example, you may have an idea to improve your customers' experience, but if it will cost more money to implement than the expected return, it might not actually be a good option. When you understand your financials, you also are in a better spot to communicate the financial value of what you provide. For example, maybe your company was able to save $10,000 due to advice you provided. This could give you bargaining power when it comes time to ask for a raise or increase your fees—especially if you can continue saving them money in the future.
- **Build emotional relationships:** Make sure you take the time to chat with your colleagues, customers, and prospects. When you get to know them on a personal level, you will understand how to best serve them. Ask about their families, interests, and

passions. Some people think small talk is a waste of time, but it really matters when forging long-term relationships. The only difference between a contact and a contract is the letter "R," which is short for "relationship." You will never get a good contract without first developing a solid relationship. People's decisions are based 80% on emotion and only 20% on logic. When you appeal to people's emotions, you win them over and have a customer for life.

- **Look for opportunity:** Keep an ear out for challenges at your organization and volunteer to help. This could mean leading a task force, conducting research, or just putting in extra hours. Don't do it with expectations for receiving anything—it's not transactional. You are simply offering to be of service to others because it's the right thing to do. Try to help people up and down the organization so you get to know more of your teammates and widen your circle of influence. This ultimately will lead to more opportunities.

COMMUNICATING VALUE

Providing value is paramount, but that's not the only thing that matters; people must also understand *why* your offering has value. One of the biggest mistakes people make in serving others is assuming they view the world through a similar lens. Typically, your clients or customers won't know anywhere near as much as you do about your products or services, which means they will have trouble identifying real quality and value unless it's pointed out to them. This isn't to say they're stupid. It's just not their job to know all of the details of your business. That's why they hired you!

Communication is a key area where people routinely drop the ball. Let's say you own a bakery and take great pride in using only the highest-quality ingredients. Unless your customers are clairvoyant, you'll need to share that information so they understand the value of your product. So you put up a sign with the single fact that you think matters most: "We only bake with butter that has 84% butterfat content." This is a great first step toward communicating value, but have you explained it in a way that makes sense to people who don't work in your industry?

Industry speak, otherwise known as "lingo," is confusing and should be avoided at all costs. Likewise, terminology for your specific department or job function may be unclear to the rest of your organization. That's why it's important to pay close attention to the way your message is worded or it's likely to go right over people's heads.

A better version of the previous message from the bakery might read, "Not all butter is created equal. We use butter with high fat content, which means less water in our pastries. Our fat-to-water ratio keeps our croissants flakey and gives our pie crusts the perfect texture."

To effectively communicate value, you have to tell people why you do things a certain way and how it affects their experience. Pointing out specific qualities helps customers notice the nuances they might otherwise take for granted. In this case, maybe customers already knew they liked your croissants and pies but they didn't quite know why. Now that you've educated them, they're better able to appreciate those qualities in your baked goods and also spot the lack of it in your competitors' products.

The same holds true for educating your team members. When you do work within your company, it's always important to communicate the value of that work so everyone understands. With the example of the bakery, the cashiers might have little knowledge of baking but receive plenty of questions and complaints about pricing. If they understand the value of the ingredients, they can communicate it to customers.

Educating others on the value you provide is not bragging. The best way to earn people's support is for them to understand why certain work matters, how it makes a difference at the company overall, and how it personally helps them.

EXERCISE

Brainstorm on the following questions and jot down your answers.

— *What problems or challenges do you solve for your colleagues? What about your customers?*

— *Do they understand the work that goes into providing this solution?*

— *Are they experiencing benefits they might not have noticed?*

— *If someone else was helping them, would their experiences or outcomes be less ideal? How?*

— *What is something you offer that nobody else does? How can you communicate that clearly to others?*

Once you understand all the ways you provide value, you need to find the right time and place to bring it to people's attention. This can be a delicate matter. Overdo it and you'll seem self-righteous or salesy; underdo it and you and your work will go unnoticed or unappreciated.

Your best option is to plan for conversations ahead of time. Devise talking points on how your work helps various departments, customers, or other stakeholders. When you have a clear idea of the right messaging, you will be well positioned to speak on those points when the opportunity arises. Particularly great times to communicate value are during team meetings, chance encounters with influential people you don't usually talk with, and during performance reviews.

REFRAMING

We've talked a lot about highlighting the most compelling aspects of the way you serve others, but we haven't yet touched on the perceived disadvantages. We all have challenges, shortcomings to overcome. However, it's important to know that just like value, disadvantages are in the eye of the beholder.

When you come upon one of the less-than-perfect aspects of your business, find a way to spin it in a positive light. This is called context reframing. For example, maybe you want to take on a specific assignment at work but you don't have a lot of experience managing that kind of project. Instead of positioning your lack of experience as a downfall, you could think about it as having a fresh perspective, as coming at the issue with a new set of eyes. You aren't stuck in the old ways of thinking, and you could see opportunities that have been overlooked in the past.

Ronald Reagan famously mastered this when he ran for office in 1980 against incumbent president Jimmy Carter. At 69 years old, Reagan would become the oldest president to take office (until Donald Trump was inaugurated at 70 years old). At the time, Reagan's age was a concern for the American people. Was he too old, tired, and past his prime? When asked about this during a televised interview, he said, "I am not going to exploit, for political purposes, my opponent's youth and inexperience."[3] He got a good laugh from the crowd, but people understood the message: he wasn't going to entertain the idea that age was a disadvantage. He artfully reframed the argument to handicap his opponent.

It's up to you whether you want to proactively bring up perceived shortcomings or stand ready to respond to them if other people bring them up to you. If one of your challenges or weaknesses could become an issue, proactively address it. This shows self-awareness, which can do wonders for strengthening others' confidence in you.

Using the previous example of age, let's say you are a decade or two younger than most of your colleagues and they make sure you don't forget it. Chances are they have more experience than you in many areas—but not all. How could you use your youth as an advantage? Do you have certain skills or knowledge that they don't?

I'm wary of being stereotypical here, but younger people who have grown up with social-media platforms tend to have a major leg up when it comes to understanding how to use them. Typically, they also tend to have an easier time leveraging those platforms for branding purposes. This can be an asset to a company as well as individuals.

For example, Instagram reels might be the perfect way to share information about your organization's products, and maybe you're the only person on staff who understands how to create that type of content. It might not seem like a big deal to you, but you could offer unique value creating reels. When your videos get hundreds—or perhaps thousands—of views, your colleagues might be shocked by the results and impressed with your work. This is how you reframe your age as a benefit.

As a leader, you will always be pulled in various directions, with people wanting different things from you. Your customers care about one matter while your boss is focused on another, and your family has a totally different agenda. It can be a real challenge! But when you're able to anticipate needs and gauge priorities, you can provide the value that matters most.

CHAPTER 8

ATTITUDE OF WHAT CAN BE

Did you know that the first electric car was created in the 1830s?[4]
It seems like such a modern invention, but the first automobiles didn't
even have gasoline engines. Electric cars didn't catch on as quickly
because no one could figure out how to make them practical. There
was little to no infrastructure for recharging batteries, drivers had to
wait overnight to recharge, and the technology was expensive. After
a while, most companies began putting all of their efforts into gas
engines, despite the reality that they depleted a nonrenewable resource
and damaged the environment.

By the early 2000s, a few companies had developed electric cars
that could go fast enough to drive on the highway, but they still couldn't
go very far without recharging, and only a tiny segment of drivers
purchased them. But when Elon Musk set his sights on improving
electric vehicles, the market started to shift. His company, Tesla, was
finally able to reinvent the electric car to make it fast, stylish, drivable

for long distances, and affordable enough that nearly a million people have purchased them since 2011.[5]

Musk embodies the entrepreneurial spirit, or what I like to call "the attitude of what can be." Instead of seeing the world how it currently is, some people envision how it could be. This attitude shapes the way they see everything—from processes, to products, to whole ways of working. Instead of accepting the status quo, they wonder how to make things better.

It's easy to see how these kinds of people make great entrepreneurs, but they also make great employees. In fact, when I'm hiring for any role, "attitude of what can be" is a key quality I always look for. Those are the people who make the business better. They come up with creative ideas, they solve long-time problems, and, quite frankly, they make my job easier. Most business owners and leaders have always appreciated having these kinds of innovators on their team, but it's become more important than ever to attract this talent and keep it.

We're living through an era of exponential change. Technology is transforming the way everything is done, and companies are finding themselves with a burgeoning need to drive innovation and stave off stagnation. To remain competitive, they need fresh perspectives, new ideas, and employees who care about improvement.

With this in mind, it's no wonder innovation has turned into a stand-alone industry. Many companies today hire expert "innovation leaders" to come in and teach employees how to think differently. They fork over thousands of dollars for keynotes, workshops, and trainings in the hopes of teaching employees to be more like Elon Musk. Some of those efforts are sure to drive change, but innovation doesn't have to be that complicated.

Innovation is so simple a child can do it. In fact, the most creative people in the world are children. Adults are often constrained by the lens of past experience. Children have the remarkable capability of viewing the world with fresh eyes. All territory is uncharted and ripe for exploration, which sets a strong framework for creative thinking. As we get older and gain more experience in the world, our brains develop thought techniques and patterns to quickly arrive at solutions. Instead of considering a wide range of possibilities, we turn to what's worked before. Quite literally, we become programmed to see things how they have always been. After a couple decades of adulthood, coming up with new ways of doing things can seem more of an arduous chore than a natural way of viewing the world. That's why it's so hard to break the status quo inside organizations and see things as they could be rather than as they are.

Luckily, innovation doesn't always mean huge accomplishments or groundbreaking inventions. It can simply be doing something slightly better than before. In Martin Lindstrom's latest book, *The Ministry of Common Sense*, he demonstrates how small changes help businesses run smoothly and save money, all while inspiring employees to enjoy their jobs.

Sometimes even the simplest ideas can lead to massive improvements. In one example, Lindstrom had partnered with several organizations to challenge employees to come up with ideas for improving their workplaces. If the idea saved money, the employee would get to pocket some of the savings. One enterprising employee had the idea to turn off all the lights on the company's manufacturing floors to save on energy expenses. Because all of the products were made by robots, they didn't actually need lights to get the work done. Flipping the switch now saves the company about $10,000 a year.

As you think about possibilities at your organization, don't overlook the easy things. Sometimes people assume that harder, more elaborate projects are more valuable and impressive, but that just isn't true when it comes to innovation. Minor tweaks can lead to vast improvements in everything from supply-chain management to customer experience and employee engagement.

I live in a somewhat-rural community outside Milwaukee, and I have a three-acre yard. I use a ride-on mower to cut the grass, but it's a time-consuming process. Ride-on mowers make wide turns, which makes it hard to cut in neat, even lines. Once I make a turn, I have to go back and reposition the mower in the right spot so I don't miss anything. That might not seem like a big deal, but it really adds up when you're cutting a lot of grass.

Enter the zero-turn mower! By putting the power in the back wheels and improving the steering capability, the mower can make on-the-spot 360-degree turns. It used to take me three hours to mow the yard. Now it only takes 45 minutes. That time is valuable to me, and I was happy to buy a new mower that could save hours of my life each summer. Think about how many other customers have the same perspective, and how much that simple idea was really worth to the lawn-mower manufacturer!

TIPS FOR IMAGINING WHAT CAN BE

Innovation may seem abstract and challenging, but the tips below will help boost your creativity so you can think differently about what's possible.

GIVE YOURSELF PARAMETERS

Have you ever watched cooking competition shows like *Top Chef*? When contestants have limited options for their challenges, they come up with creative dishes they never would have if they had total freedom to make anything they wanted. Having specific parameters helps them break out of old habits and develop fresh ideas. On the flip side, sometimes contestants are given free rein to cook any kind of dish they want, and suddenly you see the world's greatest chefs reduced to tears because they failed to edit themselves properly and develop a focused plate of food.

It seems counterintuitive, but we come up with better solutions when we have fewer options. Our minds have trouble processing abstract thought, so getting specific can be a big help. Instead of sitting down to think about innovation, try thinking about improving a certain aspect of the customer experience. Imposing restrictions on yourself will help you dial in on a single topic and go deep on solutions.

SET ASIDE TIME TO THINK

Sometimes we hear stories about how a clever idea just popped into a person's head while they were taking a shower. It's highly convenient to have a stroke of brilliance without making any effort at all, but it's rare. Unless you spend an inordinate amount of time lathering up, you'll probably have better outcomes if you set aside chunks of uninterrupted time to think.

If you have your most creative thoughts when you aren't sitting at your desk, that's fine! It's a good idea to step out of the office, get some fresh air, and rid yourself of typical distractions. Make sure to actually dedicate that time to creative thinking instead of scrolling social media. If you find yourself short on ideas, change your environment. Go sit in a park, try a new restaurant, take a different way home, or try a new activity. You never know what might inspire your next great idea. Bring a notepad, turn off your phone, and keep at it for a decent chunk of time—even if good ideas aren't exactly hitting you over the head right away. Innovation takes patience.

FIND A COMMON PROBLEM AND FIX IT

Alleviate annoyances for your colleagues or customers. This could be anything from coming up with a more intuitive way to submit expense reports to improving customer survey questions. To get good ideas for solutions, keep an ear out for complaints. When a process is messy or illogical, ask yourself whether it has to be that way. Chances are those problems could have elegant solutions.

It might take time and effort to untangle long-term issues, but the good news is that improvements will be obvious to everyone. The more widely a problem is experienced by your colleagues, the more your "fix" will be noticed and appreciated. Clever solutions can supercharge your visibility. People will talk about how nice an improvement is, and you'll become part of that conversation. This can do a lot to boost your image as a leader and show your value to the team.

LOOK TOWARD THE FUTURE

How are things changing—both inside and outside your industry? What are the trends that might affect your company's market share or the way you go about your role?

When COVID hit, people started using their homes much differently than they had in the past. As a home developer, we took note of this immediately and started thinking about how to adjust our designs and floor plans to better meet the needs of the future. My team and I started thinking about "the mudroom of the future," which would double as a place for receiving packages and wiping down groceries before bringing them to the kitchen.

Retail developers are also thinking differently about design. Pickup windows and car-side delivery spots weren't seen as incredibly useful for most businesses, but they're currently en vogue and probably will stay that way for a while. Why go inside to get your latte, pizza, or dry cleaning if it's even easier to use a pickup window or have someone drop it out to you?

EMBRACE TECHNOLOGY

Some of the biggest innovations around the world relate to using technology in different ways. A recent change we've seen is that restaurants and bars finally have gone digital. By scanning a QR code on your phone, you can easily view a menu and pay for your meal. This technology had been around since 1994, but most of us hadn't heard about it until about a decade ago.[6] Even then, it was mostly used on things like flyers and bus-stop ads. It hadn't occurred to people that QR codes could find a nice home inside high-end dining establishments. Now that we all see how convenient it is for both customers and servers, it's doubtful most restaurants will ever go back to wiping our greasy fingerprints off laminated menus.

MIMIC OTHER INDUSTRIES

I tend to look toward the auto industry for inspiration because it has a lot of similarities to the home-building industry. As an example, customers can get many different customizations to their new car—or new home. A few years ago, I noticed that the auto industry started to change how they approached customizations. Instead of inviting customers to pick out exactly what they wanted from a laundry list of options, they started offering packages. With package A, customers could elect to get ABC options; with package B, they could opt for XYZ.

At first, I wondered why auto manufacturers had chosen to go that route, but I soon realized they had made an informed and strategic decision. Customers love personalization, but it's time consuming to sell and even harder to manage during the manufacturing process. Switching to packaged options would still enable customers to select different features, but it would streamline the process and make it easier for the automotive company to deliver. In other words, it was a great idea for saving time and money while still giving customers a chance to pick what they want. In fact, it was my inspiration for pulling back on my company's customization options, as discussed in Chapter 4. I saw what worked for the auto industry and found that it also could be a wildly successful strategy for building homes.

My company is in the process of mimicking another innovation from the auto industry. Drivers have been syncing their smartphones to their cars for years, and now we're doing it with homes. The number of smart features available for homes is increasing exponentially. We use smart-home technology so people can control the temperature, lock and unlock doors, and monitor security cameras with just the touch of a button.

PARTNER WITH THOSE DIFFERENT THAN YOU

Research has shown that homogeneous teams do not perform as well as diverse teams. When you work with people who have similar backgrounds, life experiences, and perspectives, you tend to look at problems in similar ways. You are more likely to come up with the same kinds of solutions while overlooking key opportunities for improvement. But when you partner with those who differ from you in a variety of ways, that's when the magic happens.

I love teaming younger employees with employees who have more life experience. Together, they combine their unique perspectives to come up with creative solutions that neither could have dreamt up individually.

Matching up people who work in different departments is also a good way to inspire teammates to view the company through a different lens. Cross-departmental brainstorming sessions can be incredibly fruitful when it comes to developing fresh solutions.

COMMUNICATING YOUR IDEAS

When you have an attitude of what can be, you'll come up with all kinds of innovative ideas to make a powerful impact at your organization. However, to execute your ideas, you'll need to gain buy-in from your team. People might not initially understand how beneficial small changes can be without experiencing it for themselves.

I see this a lot with homeowners when I am explaining smart-home technology. If they haven't lived in a smart home, they don't know what they're missing and don't really see the value of opting for this upgrade. After telling a few buyers about the technology and getting less-than-enthusiastic responses, I realized people might not understand all of the situations where it would be useful.

I started using stories to explain how it would make their lives easier and give them peace of mind. If they ever left home and wondered if they remembered to close the garage, they wouldn't have to stress all day about their bikes getting stolen or waste time driving home to check. Instead, they could just check their phone. If they wanted to see if their kids made it home from school on time, they wouldn't have to call or text—they could just check the app. When I learned to explain the benefits with a story that showed how the innovation would improve customers' lives, the difference in response was remarkable.

Your offer can make total sense on paper, but the way it's delivered will impact whether your customers sign on. To get people on board with new solutions, play to their emotions rather than just their sense of logic. People make decisions based on how they feel about something deep down in their gut. Does it make them feel happy, excited, worried, bored? All of those things matter.

Another key thing to remember is how personality and learning type influence the way people see the world. Before you pitch a new idea to your boss or a client, refer back to Chapter 3 and think about what's important to them. Are they concerned with saving time (a hallmark of the high-direct personality)? If so, make sure you highlight how your proposal will increase efficiency—and make sure to deliver your message in a concise way! On the flip side, if you're communicating with a high-calculating type, details are a must. You'll need to do all your research, lay it out in a clear and organized way, and share it because they will definitely read every word! When you present your ideas for innovative changes in the "languages" that other people speak, you will have much more success gaining buy-in and support.

Take time to imagine what *can be* to hack your growth at any organization. Whether it's your first day on the job or you've already built a multibillion-dollar company, work hard to be the kind of person who never settles. When performance starts to slow, dip, or plateau, look for ways to make things better. Embrace that feeling of restlessness or boredom that comes from lack of change. This is the kind of person I love working with—and the kind of person I strive to be every day.

CHAPTER 9

MAINTAINING AN UNENDING HUNGER TO SUCCEED

My dad was my inspiration. His business was his third baby, and he cared about it almost as much as he cared for my brother and me. Dad dedicated every day to doing the best possible job for his customers, and that showed through his actions.

I'll never forget how he would drive out to the houses we were building with a bucket of nails in tow. And as the tradespeople were home relaxing, their feet up after a hard day's work, he would be checking out the floors and pounding in extra nails to make sure everything was solid. Customers never saw that, and neither did the other people who worked for the company. But I took notice, and it made a profound impact on how I think about my career.

Through my dad's actions, I saw that success takes hard work and sacrifice. He made it look easy, like a duck gliding gracefully over the water, paddling like crazy just below the surface. He built a thriving company because he was so driven. He wanted to be successful, so he kept pushing. In his eyes, there always was more to be done. I've taken those lessons to heart.

I've also noticed a few things about "the greats." Whether they're Olympic athletes, professional musicians, or high-performing corporate executives, they all have natural talent—but more than that, they have an unending hunger to succeed. Ability is what separates them from their peers early on, but their intrinsic motivation is what drives them forward. They're fascinated by their craft, and they simply put in the effort to research, learn, and practice more than anyone else. Sometimes it might look like they just showed up and got lucky, but few people, if any, will ever know the true amount of effort and willpower necessary to succeed at the highest levels.

You could choose to look at this two ways. The first is to be discouraged by what lies ahead: hard work. But chances are you've already known that's in your future. The second (and better) way to view this personal growth journey is to take comfort in knowing that your hard work will pay off. The people who want something the most are usually the ones who get it, simply because they refuse to give up. If you become a person who refuses to give up, or settle for anything less than what you really want, what could you achieve?

Finishing this book marks the beginning of your growth-hacking journey! The principles, tips, and tricks I've shared are universal. Some of the information may be straightforward, but consistently executing on all of these skill sets can take a lifetime to master. Whether you're an employee, freelancer, or business owner, focus on what matters most to take your career to the next level.

Here are a few final words of advice as you move forward on your own:

LEADERS ARE LEARNERS

Never underestimate the power of knowledge. Whether you're at the beginning of your career or retirement is on the horizon, always work to grow and improve. Set aside 20 minutes each day to read an enriching book or magazine article. If that sounds too difficult to fit into your schedule, try audiobooks and listen while you drive, run on the treadmill, or unload the dishwasher. Sign up for webinars or events in your industry and subscribe to email newsletters that have worthwhile information. Whenever you learn something interesting, take notes and reflect. Start a journal or a notes document on your computer and fill it with your ideas and inspirations. These notes will benefit you today and many years down the road. You'll soon find that the little tidbits of information you pick up here and there change how you view the world.

PUT YOUR BEST FACE FORWARD

At your best, you are a person who helps others, inspires greatness, and makes the world a better place. But if you don't take care of yourself, you won't be positioned to present your best self to the world. That, in itself, would be a disservice to the people around you. That's why it shouldn't feel selfish to focus on self-care. Prioritizing your own well-being charges your batteries so that you're better able to contribute to your colleagues, family, and community.

LIVE ON YOUR OWN TERMS

You only get one life. Don't waste it trying to please others. If you sense a disconnect between your current reality and your dream life, make changes focused on long-term happiness. What would you do differently if you weren't constantly seeking the approval of friends, family members, and connections? Take baby steps to bridge the gap between where you are now and where you want to be. If you strive to live your best life every day, good people in your sphere will naturally approve, flocking together to help lift you higher.

WORK FOR A SECURE FUTURE

When we're young and healthy, we have boundless energy. We all hope to keep this up in our later years, but we never know what the future will hold. That's why it's smart to work hard when you can and save for your future. Having some savings built up also can provide you with freedom when you need it most. If you ever need to walk away from a job that is crushing your soul, you can do it—even if you don't have anything else lined up.

IT'S NEVER TOO LATE

Don't ever think that your dream has already passed you by. I recently interviewed a man in his 60s. He just launched a new business that he had been thinking about for decades. His first journey into entrepreneurship was about 30 years ago, and like many new businesses, it went under. The man thought of himself as a failure for a long time, and he resisted the urge to try again. He plugged along for years, working for others and denying his passion. But after three decades, he finally decided to give it another shot, and he couldn't be happier. If you feel like you've missed the boat on pursuing your dream, ask whether it's truly impossible to go after it now. Chances are that it isn't too late after all.

SHARE YOUR KNOWLEDGE

Teach others what you have learned and give back to the world to make it a better place. You could publish articles, maintain a helpful Twitter account, or host live Q&As. There are an infinite number of ways to contribute. Let your colleagues know that you're happy to answer questions and help whenever possible, or even serve as a mentor or ally. When you get to a certain point in your career, reaching back and helping others becomes a rewarding responsibility. Put goodness into the world and goodness will come back to you!

IDEAS FOR MAINTAINING AN UNENDING HUNGER TO SUCCEED

Identify:	What do you want to be remembered for?
Determine milestones:	What do you need to accomplish to reach your goals?
Explore skill sets:	What skill sets do you need to tackle the tasks ahead?
Affirmations daily:	What is your mantra (e.g., I am a highly organized person, I radiate positivity, etc.)?
Seek out education:	Where can you improve? (Allocate 20 minutes each day to enrichment: read books, listen to industry-related podcasts, take online courses, etc.)

LEGACY

Have you ever thought about your life and been able to pinpoint one moment in time that altered your trajectory? For me, thinking about my legacy motivated me to look at how I could impact my life in a meaningful way.

I was listening to a keynote speech at a conference and the speaker started talking about legacy. I honestly had never given it much thought. He asked us what people would say about us if we died that very day. It was a compelling, albeit morbid, question. After the keynote ended, I couldn't shake it. I thought about legacy the next day and the day after that. Finally, I realized that I couldn't stop thinking about it. Perhaps because I was uncomfortable with the answer. What *would* people say about me if I suddenly died?

I felt I was a good husband and father and that I'd done fairly well in my career, but I wondered what I had done that was worth talking about after I was gone. I closed my eyes and imagined my own wake: *David was a good builder ... What a nice guy ... He ran his business well.* What an underwhelming tribute! I wanted more than that. I wanted my life to be about more. I knew I needed to make a major change. I wasn't chasing fame or fortune; I wanted to be known for doing something that mattered and for making the world a better place. That's when my outlook shifted.

This was right around the time when Operation Finally Home found me, and I started taking the actions necessary to become the person I had always wanted to be. Thinking about my legacy gave me a greater sense of urgency for doing philanthropic work *right now*, rather than planning on doing it "someday." It finally hit home that tomorrow is never guaranteed and we have to live each day as though it were our last.

A beautiful new home we donated in 2017 to Army Specialist Philip Olson as part of Operation Finally Home (Photo courtesy of Operation Finally Home.).

A ribbon-cutting celebration in 2019 for Army Sergeant First Class Tyson Cole. (Photo courtesy of Operation Finally Home.)

I dove into my work with Operation Finally Home and felt my passion unleashed. It wasn't always smooth sailing, and there were plenty of setbacks. For instance, while digging the basement in our first home for the project, we found truckloads of buried garbage. It caused a major setback, and we had to pay to get it hauled away. Almost immediately after starting the project, we were over budget by thousands of dollars!

I thought about all the builders who did not want to lead this project because of the financial risks, and for a brief moment, I wondered whether they were right. Had I taken on more than I should have? What if the only legacy I created with Operation Finally Home was that of a failed project leader?

To get back to a positive mindset, I focused on the big picture and all the good we were doing. I hit the reset button on my thought patterns and knew I was on the right path. I just had to work harder and demonstrate resilience.

My team and I decided to do a donation drive with the local fire department. This consisted of us standing near a major intersection in 95-degree weather with plastic buckets to collect spare change from drivers. We were all shocked to count more than $9,000 in cash by the end of the day.

This kind of generosity made me realize that when it comes to legacy, we all want to leave the world a better place than we found it. We all hope to be the kind of leaders who stand up, do the right thing, and help others in need.

As you think about your own career growth, focus on giving back to the world. You will find a greater purpose in life that will inspire you to do—and become—more than you were.

This book has given you all you need to drive exponential growth. Now, all you have to do is turn your knowledge into action. Take time to think about your legacy. What do you want to be known for? Use that positive energy and get to work on yourself. You deserve it! Go back through the advice in this book and put it to use. Make sure you also check out the resources in the following section. In no time at all, you'll see how small changes can make a huge difference in your life and the lives of others. Become that shining light in the dark.

DAVID BELMAN
LEADERSHIP GROWTH HACKS

LEGACY BUILDER

GRATITUDE

Today I am grateful for...

- [ ] _____
- [ ] _____
- [ ] _____

GOALS

I will...

- [ ] _____
- [ ] _____
- [ ] _____

AFFIRMATIONS

I am...

- [ ] _____
- [ ] _____
- [ ] _____
- [ ] _____

RESOURCES

As our journey through this book comes to a close, I hope that this isn't goodbye! Visit www.davidbelman.net/resources/ to find a variety of resources and ways to stay connected.

DOWNLOADABLES:

- *Goals worksheet*
- *Time study*
- *Personality determination*
- *Overcoming fear*
- *Legacy builder*
- *Personal brand worksheet*
- *Affirmation list*

THE YOUNG GUNS MOVEMENT

As an entrepreneur or professional, you no longer need to seek permission to authentically speak what you believe in. Stand out and share what makes you unique so you can attract the business and collaborators that align with your point of view.

The Young Guns group inspires, motivates, and encourages professionals to be authentic and courageously share their vision with the world.

Together, we collaborate to keep up with the speed of innovation with respect to personal branding, social media, business creation, and differentiation, among many other important topics. The Young Guns movement hosts quarterly virtual summits with top thought leaders to help sharpen your skills and meet other action-orientated risk takers that you can create new opportunities with.

Visit www.younggunsevent.com for more information.

YGTV

If you dive into the stories of people that changed the world, you'll find one common thread: They relentlessly pursued their vision and didn't give in to the status quo. Inspired by the innovators that have come before, the Young Guns Movement has created a new platform for free thinkers and action-oriented entrepreneurs to share their vision and break the rules of business.

The Young Guns Movement has launched YGTV, a new business channel presenting original programming that features inspirational and impactful content to help entrepreneurs scale their business and personal brand. The channel features local CEOs and business leaders alongside the area's hottest keynote speakers and business rebels.

Watch and subscribe here: www.youtube.com/c/YoungGunsTV.

HOME BUILDING HERO PODCAST

Whether you are building, buying, designing, or renovating, this podcast provides all the information you need to make great decisions for your home. As the host, I lead interesting discussions with all kinds of people on the latest new home designs, styles, and industry trends to help make you the hero of your new home. New episodes air every Monday, Wednesday, and Friday. Subscribe so you don't miss an episode! https://anchor.fm/homebuildinghero

Website: www.homebuildinghero.com

Twitter: @building_hero and #homebuildinghero

OPERATIONFINALLYHOME.ORG

OPERATION FINALLY HOME

Military heroes sacrifice everything for our country. Many of them return from combat injured and unable to work. The government provides disability compensation, but retirement pay isn't enough to cover housing and basic needs and keep food on the table for a family. When I learned how little our country's veterans actually receive for sacrificing life and limb, I was heartbroken. Veterans have given the most for our freedom, and we should do all we can to give back.

My organization, Belman Homes, has partnered with Operation Finally Home to give away a mortgage-free home to a wounded veteran every year. Please consider joining us! We are always fundraising and looking for more volunteers. If you'd like to make a monetary contribution to the homes we build in Wisconsin, you can do so at www.OperationFinallyHome.org/Wisconsin.

If you're interested in volunteering your time or getting your business involved, please contact me directly at david@belmanhomes.com. Every small action makes a tremendous difference, and I am grateful for any level of involvement or support!

SPEAKING

If your company or group is in need of some leadership inspiration, or if you would like to explore the concepts from this book on a deeper level, I'd love to help! Check out my website for more information: www.davidbelman.net

ACKNOWLEDGEMENTS

Writing a book was something I always wanted to accomplish but continually put off. Ultimately, it took a lot of headspace, patience, and incredible people to help get me across this finish line!

Paul M. Neuberger, thank you for picking up the phone and inviting me on the Young Guns journey with you. That call ignited me and helped me get into this process.

A special thank you to Amelia Forczak. I don't know how you do it, but my gratitude goes out to you for helping me organize all the madness in my head and keeping me focused throughout this process. I could not have done this without you. You are a true professional.

Michaela Alexis, thank you for your courage and for showing me that it's okay to be vulnerable.

Sometimes the right people come into your life at the exact right time. Chris Penasa, I would not be where I am today without your guidance. Thank you for all the conversations, wisdom, and friendship over the years. The force is strong with you!

Shay Rowbottom, thank you for dropping so much down-to-earth wisdom and for being unapologetically authentic.

I have been blessed to have a fantastic team at Belman Homes. You are more than just my team; you are my family. We have been through a lot and accomplished a ton, and I am grateful that you have stuck with me through thick and thin. There hasn't been one thing we set out to do that we haven't accomplished.

A special thank-you to Ed Brzozowski for the amazing photography and to Serendipity Labs for letting me have the run of the place to capture these images.

Thank you to the Operation Finally Home team for your love, positivity, and support. You created an amazing, life-changing cause for some of the most deserving people on Earth, and I am proud to be a part of that.

Taking a few abstract ideas and creating a picture is incredibly hard. Claire Lacy, thank you for taking some broad ideas and painting them into a clear vision for the book.

Morgan Markowski, thank you for reaching out to me of all people for guidance. Your exponential growth validates that the information in this book really works.

Chris Peters, you were able to take some messy constructs and make them technically sound. I appreciate your keen eye.

Mom, thank you for instilling leadership principles in me at a young age. I still remember all those lessons of confidence: "Be a leader, not a follower." You pushed me.

Dad, thank you for making me the man that I have become. I am incredibly lucky to have had you as my parent but also to work beside you for so many years. I know that you are looking down on me proudly, and I will continue to carry on the legacy.

Lastly, my deepest gratitude goes out to my wife, Susan. Thank you for putting up with me. You have been with me through my best and my worst, sticking by me and keeping my head from getting lost in the clouds.

NOTES

1— "Law of attraction (New Thought)," Wikipedia, accessed September 28, 2020, https://en.wikipedia.org/wiki/Law_of_attraction_(New_Thought).

2— "The Secret (book)," Wikipedia, accessed September 28, 2020, https://en.wikipedia.org/wiki/The_Secret_(book).

3— "Reagan and the age issue," Youtube, accessed October 30, 2020, https://www.youtube.com/watch?v=fJhCjMfRndk&feature=youtu.be&t=28s.

4— Kevin A. Wilson, "Worth the Watt: A Brief History of the Electric Car, 1830 to Present," March 15, 2018, https://www.caranddriver.com/features/g15378765/worth-the-watt-a-brief-history-of-the-electric-car-1830-to-present/?slide=1.

5— "Tesla, Inc.," Wikipedia, accessed September 28, 2020, https://en.wikipedia.org/wiki/Tesla,_Inc.#:~:text=going%20after%20it.%22-,Vehicle%20Sales,2012%20totaled%20over%20891%2C000%20units.

6— "History of QR Code," QRCode.com, accessed October 29, 2020, https://www.qrcode.com/en/history/#:~:text=In%201994%2C%20DENSO%20WAVE%20(then,placed%20on%20high%2Dspeed%20reading.

ABOUT THE AUTHOR

David Belman believes that there is nothing more rewarding than witnessing someone come into their own, break through challenges, and evolve into a true leader. A successful entrepreneur, philanthropist, and enthusiastic mentor to emerging leaders,

David is passionate about helping others reach their full potential. He shares his insights with the world by speaking to growing companies

and inspiring emerging leaders, helping them find the bigger picture and release their true potential.

As the owner of Belman Homes and a leader in the building industry, David advocates on behalf of builders at the local, state, and national levels. He and his firm have won numerous awards, including Top Choice Award for Best Builder in Milwaukee six times in a row (2014–2020), 2017 Waukesha Freeman Citizen of the Year, 2020 Waukesha County Emerging Leader Award, 2017 Builder of the Year from the Metropolitan Builders Association, 2014 Rising Star Award from the Wisconsin Builders Association, and 2017 National Association of Home Builders Young Professional of the Year Award. In addition to these honors, David and his firm were awarded North American awards for the 2014 Best Young Entrepreneur for North America and 2015 Best Company Culture Award for North America from the Business Excellence Forum.

David cares deeply about philanthropy, and he is best known for giving away mortgage-free homes to wounded war heroes in Wisconsin. He works within the community to raise funds and materials, and as of 2021, this massive undertaking has provided six free homes to deserving veterans.